An Intelligent Organization

An Intelligent
Organization

Integrating Performance, Competence and Knowledge Management

Pentti Sydänmaanlakka

CAPSTONE

First published 2002 by
Capstone Publishing Limited (a Wiley company)
8 Newtec Place
Magdalen Road
Oxford OX4 1RE
United Kingdom
http://www.capstoneideas.com

British Library Cataloguing in Publication Data
A CIP catalogue record for this book is available from the British Library

ISBN 1-84112-048-0

Typeset in 11/16 pt Minion by
Sparks Computer Solutions Ltd, Oxford
http://www.sparks.co.uk
Printed and bound by
T.J. International Ltd, Padstow, Cornwall

This book is printed on acid-free paper

Contents

Preface   *vii*

Introduction   1
1   **Organisational Learning**   7
    Learning as a competitive factor and means of survival
    What is learning?
    Levels of learning
    Learning skills of the organisation
    Learning and feedback
    Learning and change
    How to support learning by doing

2   **Performance Management**   55
    Continuous improvement of performance as an objective
    The viewpoint of the organisation, individual and environment
    Planning and development discussions
    Daily leadership and planning meetings
    Connections to other human resource management processes
    Summary and critical success factors

3   **Competence Management**   97
    Continuous improvement of competence as an objective
    Strategic management
    Core competence as a framework
    Competence management in practice
    Individual competence
    Summary: what did we learn?

4   Knowledge Management   **133**
Continuous application of new knowledge as an objective
What is knowledge management?
Knowledge management in practice
Intellectual capital and its measurement
Summary and conclusions

5   An Intelligent Organisation   **165**
Towards an intelligent organisation
The features of an intelligent organisation
Management in an intelligent organisation
Human resource management in an intelligent organisation
On the way towards an intelligent organisation
The ideal organisation of the future

Glossary   *197*
References   *205*
Appendices   *211*
Index   *231*

Preface

This book is based on my personal experiences. I have also actively followed the literature and research in this field, from which I have sourced many valuable ideas. During the last five years I have done a lot of lecturing on these topics in Finland and other countries. I have found trying to train other people almost the only way, and a very efficient one, of teaching myself in my hectic work environment. As I will discuss in the book, when you have to explain something to others you have to completely understand and internalise the topic yourself. During and after these presentations, I was repeatedly given feedback from my audiences and it became clear that these topics would have interest to a much wider audience. That is why I have written this book.

The ideas in this book had their genesis in work I have done with many different people. I know that I cannot name all of them but I must mention a couple of people who have had a great impact on my thinking over the last few years through their books, thoughts and being. They are Leif Edvidson, Klaus Lurse, Michael Marquardt, Andrew Mayo, Ikujiro Nonaka, Sudhanshu Palsule, Jagdish Parikh, Charles Savage, Peter Senge and Karl Erick Sveiby. A great thanks to all of them and the many others who have taught me something valuable about the way an organisation learns.

However, it is not their responsibility if I have misunderstood something.

This book is dedicated to the work done to overcome the problem of drugs abuse. Drugs are a problem the magnitude of which we still probably don't understand enough. The use of drugs has increased enormously almost everywhere over the last ten years.

Drugs abuse presents a difficult problem in so many ways. Not least because it is a crime against humanity. The highest level of human achievement is being able to develop our consciousness. It is something we should cherish and maintain throughout our lives. But the misuse of drugs prevents the development of consciousness, creates an artificial reality, and alienates us from our inner selves. We all need to fight against this dehumanising process of psychological alienation.

The growing misuse of drugs among the young is especially sad. It will require us adults to focus more of our attention on the youth of today. We should not leave them alone. And in order that we can afford more time with our children, we must increase the efficiency of our organisations. Those of us that work in businesses spend most of our time in our organisations. And the ultimate purpose of this book is to find ways to improve the operations of our organisations so we can also do other things than just work. We don't live to work well. We work to live well.

Espoo 13.1.2002

Pentti Sydänmaanlakka

Introduction

Wherever we are employed, the likelihood is that we are working long hours and dedicating a huge amount of our time to the organisation. That makes it particularly tragic that so many organisations are operating inefficiently. But the pressures grow by the day, both from internal sources and from the external global environment. So it is imperative that we learn to continuously develop our operations to enable our organisation to stay competitive. And we need to do that in an intelligent way, by taking into account the perspective of the individuals, the teams and all the personnel that form the organisation. A competent and motivated personnel is ultimately the only permanent competitive edge that a company can achieve.

The purpose of my book is to find answers to how we can develop the ideal organisation for the future, one that is efficient, capable of learning, and sensitive to the well-being of its personnel all at the same time. The competition gets tougher every day but that is simply something to which we must now adapt. In practical terms that means the profits of our business must continuously improve to allow us to survive in an ever more unforgiving economic climate. But public organisations, who don't have the same profit motive, also need to work ever more efficiently. I use the term organisation to describe all the different kinds of organisations in which we work, and they are all in equal need of the intelligent development of their processes.

Since the profits of our organisation must continuously improve if it is to survive, then the performance of the organisation and its personnel needs to improve at the same rate. And that performance depends on the competence we have in our organisation, our teams and individuals. It consists of knowledge, skills, attitudes, experience, and contacts, as well as the organisation's processes, operational models and culture. Competence management has become a success factor for our organisation.

The contents of the competence needed in a fast changing environment also changes fast. In the organisation of the future, competence in itself will no longer be a guarantee of success, but instead it will be the competence development process that becomes a critical success factor. And that will require us to really understand what learning is all about. We will have to understand the learning process on individual, team and organisational levels. Individual learning is not sufficient by itself and we will have to learn together and simultaneously as a team. Often it is the team that becomes the basic unit for learning in today's organisation.

The purpose of my book is to answer the following questions:

- How can we improve the organisation's capacity to learn?
- How can we manage and systematically develop the competence needed in the organisation?
- How can we improve the performance of the personnel and the entire organisation?
- How can we achieve better business results?
- How will we manage in the ever more competitive global business environment?

And, perhaps most importantly, we will look at how to achieve all these objectives at the same time as thinking about the viewpoint of individuals. That means integrating the efficiency, the renewal and the well-being of the organisation.

I attempt to answer these questions from my own narrow viewpoint. I believe that by improving the processes for performance, competence and knowledge management, we will be able to find concrete answers to these questions. And that, in turn, will enable us to advance on our way towards an intelligent organisation. Figure 1 shows how to enhance the competitiveness of the organisation without ignoring the individual.

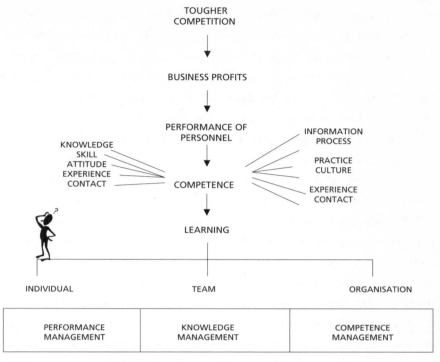

Fig. 0.1 Enhancing the competitiveness of the organisation

There's an immediate problem with using the concepts of performance, competence and knowledge management. They are management fads, much chewed over around the water-cooler, but rarely understood or properly applied. So the goal of this book is to try to clarify, pinpoint and simplify the confusing array of concepts which we encounter every day. I will attempt to describe these processes in practical terms based on the experience I have gained during the past twenty years. And I will try to reflect on and understand deeper issues which I have personally tried to apply in practice. I hope the outcome will be a somewhat more systematic picture of these issues that can help us develop the ideal organisation of the future. That should be enough to justify this book at a time when literally thousands roll off the presses every week.

The content of the book is divided into five chapters, which can be read independently but I would recommend the reader follows the order. In the first chapter, we will try to understand what organisational learning is all about – defining it as the ability of the organisation to renew itself by changing its values, practices and processes. We will study the learning process on an individual, team and organisational level and determine that renewal is about the capacity to continuously acquire new competencies and apply them together. It is very important to understand the learning process in order to be able to support it as efficiently as possible.

The second chapter deals with performance management. Performance management links objective setting, reviewing and coaching, evaluation, and development as integrated elements in an on-going process. It is all about continuously improving the organisation's performance by developing the individuals and the teams. Performance management means simply that everyone knows their tasks and individual objectives, what kind of competence is expected of them, and that they will get enough coaching and feedback. The most important concrete tools in performance management are planning and development discussions. But it is important to understand the philosophy and basics of performance management in a wider context when trying to conduct development discussions with staff. Too often, an organisation has the theory in place but gets the practice wrong. The problem is often simply that the real purpose of the exercise has not been fully understood and they have not been integrated into the other management systems of the organisation. Performance management is, in my opinion, the most important human resource management process, forming the foundation for many other processes. Special attention should therefore be paid to make sure that it works in the organisation.

The third chapter deals with competence management. Competence management means defining the core competencies and other necessary skills to achieve the vision, strategy and objectives of the company. Once identified, it is all about developing these competencies systematically. Most people have come across the competence management concept over the last decade. The giddying pace of change means competence has become an issue of survival for both the organisation and the individuals. But the implementation of competence management has created plenty of problems, not least the confusion that stems from uncertainty about some of the first principles. What, for example, are the core competence areas of the organisation? What are the competencies needed? How should they be measured? A lot of organisations have allowed themselves to get confused about competence management but still try to set themselves concrete goals in that muddled state. This chapter explores how these challenges can be met in practice.

The fourth chapter deals with knowledge management. Knowledge management is a process where we create, capture, store, share and apply knowledge. The goal is the rapid application of knowledge in decision-making. It is the newest one of these three processes but it has become an ever more frequent subject of discussion over the past few years. It is still a novelty in many organisations, which means it gets a lot of attention but produces very little in the way of real action. But it is an extremely important process that needs to be properly understood and implemented in today's knowledge companies.

I have often asked at my lectures how many companies consistently use an effective process for performance, competence and knowledge management. On average, the answers have suggested that 75 percent of organisations use a performance management system (which usually does not work very well), 50 percent are using a competence management process and about 25 percent are experimenting with some sort of knowledge management process.

The fifth chapter discusses what makes a truly intelligent organisation. An intelligent organisation takes a long-term approach to the competitiveness challenge, competence and the needs of its personnel. It learns quickly and efficiently. This chapter describes how we can develop the ideal organisation of the future, presenting some concrete steps and a framework to evaluate the current state of our own organisation. The chapter also contains a summary of how we might be able to implement the performance, competence and knowledge management processes in our ideal organisation and it describes how we can integrate them into a single renewed performance management process.

One of the general principles of an intelligent organisation is its simplicity. It aspires to reduce, crystallise, focus, and see issues in their entirety. The endless stream of short-lived management fads creates more confusion than clarity. It often leaves us wondering what is happening in our organisation, in our industry and in the wider environment. An intelligent organisation circumvents all that muddle.

It can balance the drive for efficiency, learning and well-being. And it is that balance that enables it to constantly renew itself and foresee change. An intelligent organisation learns faster than the speed at which the surrounding environment is changing, which means it can cope with flux. The company's most important resource is its personnel, who combine to produce collective competence, commitment and well-being. An intelligent organisation is built for those people and does not expect the people to have to adapt to the organisation. That's the way it should be in all organisations. We spend a huge part of our lives in different organisations so they should be ideal places to work and allow us to grow comprehensively as human beings.

The process of building an intelligent organisation is not necessarily an easy one. It demands a radical change in the way we think. We have to build a new framework that will help us to perceive the world differently and to see just how the individual, the team and the whole organisation interrelate with one another to form an intelligent entity. We have to challenge our present beliefs (paradigms). We have to renew our thinking. In today's changing environment we need to dismantle our present beliefs and create new values.

And these new organisations will display intelligence itself in a new form. It will be composed of intellectual, emotional and intuitive intelligence, together forming a creative intelligence. And this creative intelligence will help us to create a bright future where enlightened organisations will make it good to work and, correspondingly, even better to live.

Chapter 1
Organisational Learning

'There was a time when the prime business of business was to make a profit and product. There is now a prior, prime business, which is to become an effective learning organisation. Not that profit and product are no longer important, but without continual learning, profits and products will no longer be possible. Hence the strange thought: **the business of business is learning** *– and all else will follow.'*

Harrison Owen: *Riding the Tiger;*
Doing Business in a Transforming World

Relentless and breathless change has made effective organisational learning an imperative for business survival. At the very least, it is a serious competitive advantage. To quote Harrison Owen: the core business of business is learning. In this chapter I will explore just why learning has become such an important feature of the modern business landscape. I will explain what learning really means and how to describe the learning process.

I will be looking at its essential components – experience, evaluation, understanding and application – and define the building blocks that will be essential to the fast renewal of organisations. I will also describe the different learning styles and obstacles of learning, types of learning and learning skills and facilities.

Learning takes place on three different levels; on an individual level, on a team level and on an organisational level. I will look at how they are related to one another. I will also discuss how feedback is connected to learning and how we can manage change. We have to get to grips with these elements to be able to understand organisational learning.

Once we have mastered the principles of learning, on an individual, team and organisational level, we can look at how it can be supported. That means enhancing its effectiveness with the help of performance, competence, and knowledge management. They are at the heart of organisational learning. They are partly overlapping, but each of them has its own role and geography. The starting point for performance management is the job and tasks and it relates mainly to the individual. Competence management starts from the vision and strategy and focuses mainly on the organisation. And knowledge management relates to the knowledge and experience of the organisation and works chiefly on the team level. Figure 1.1 illustrates all this. They do not exist in isolation from each other. They overlap in some areas. And they are all fundamental to the learning process.

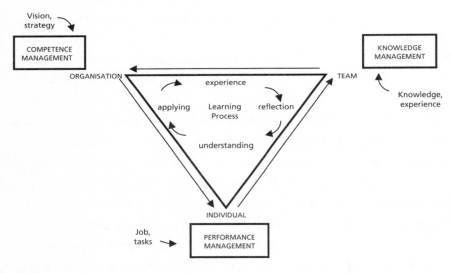

Fig. 1.1   Performance, competence and knowledge management supporting organisational learning

Learning as a competitive factor and means of survival

We live in a turbulent world in which change is the only certainty. The propellent forces, like technology, are so great it is often hard to make sense of what is going on. But if we do not understand change, it is difficult for us to control it. Managing this turbulence requires a new kind of approach and analysis both by the individual and the organisation. We have to put up with more and more insecurity and uncertainty, which demand of us new levels of flexibility. But if we can accept the chaos created by change, we can adapt to it and even 'manage' it. Management means that we have to try to anticipate the change, conform to it and control it, although we may often not be able to understand it analytically.

Change factors

What is it that is changing then? **The amount of knowledge** increases exponentially all the time and human capital grows ever more important. Scientific and technological knowledge will double almost every five years. **Technological change** is the main reason for knowledge senility. It has been predicted there will be more technical change within the next 10–20 years than during the whole of world history so far! **Globalisation** is making big inroads everywhere. We can already see now how we live in a continuously contracting 'world village'. And **competition** is more pervasive and intense than ever before. It means that companies are in a continuous state of change. **The economic and political environment** changes continuously. The changes are fast and difficult to anticipate. **The social environment and conditions** change. Present values are questioned and re-evaluated. The average age of the working population increases and competence requirements get more demanding. Pressures in working life are growing inescapably quickly. So much so, in fact, that there is a danger that our healthy work community is beginning to sicken. And we face new challenges every day from the pressures on **the environment** and our **ecological well-being**. These are just a few examples of changes that we face every day.

All this change demands a lot from an organisation. In a stable competitive environment a relatively simple and mechanical organisation is enough for success. But in a quickly changing and unpredictable environment success requires continuous change and renewal – in short, organisational learning. For the organisation learning has become a real competitive advantage. And it brings with it a lot of new challenges. The organisation won't thrive without the ability to renew itself, without speed, flexibility and the capacity to innovate.

Continuous change also demands a lot from the individual. Work has become a continuous learning process for us all. Consider all the different types of change indentified by Hammer and Champy (1993). The following list of ten issues is a summary of the sort of changes that we face in working organisations:

1 Work units change – from functional departments to process teams.
2 Jobs change – from simple tasks to multi-dimensional work.
3 The roles of the people change – from controlled to empowered.
4 Job preparation changes – from training to education.
5 The focus of performance and compensation changes – from activity to results.
6 Advancement criteria change – from performance to ability.
7 Values change – from protective to productive.
8 Managers change – from supervisors to coaches.
9 Organisational structures change – from hierarchical to flat.
10 Executives change – from scorekeepers to leaders.

Marquardt and Berger (2001) have produced another list of the major changes underway in the workplace. They focus on eight forces that will dominate the business world of the twenty-first century:

1 Globalisation and the global economy; we have really entered the Global Age.
2 Computer technology; the speed and impact of technology continues to accelerate.
3 Radical transformation of world of work; how we are working is changing continuously.
4 Increased power and demands on the customer.

5 Emergence of knowledge and learning as a company's and country's greatest assets.
6 New roles and expectations of workers; deeper search for meaning at work.
7 Biotechnology is widely forecast as being the dominant force of the twenty-first century.
8 Speed of change; moving from a Newtonian world to a quantum world of chaos.

If we needed a reminder of the intensity of change in the modern world just think about the profound impact the terrorist attacks in the US on September 11 had on the way we look at geopolitics. Turbulence is a state in which the speed and complexity of change surpass our ability to understand that change analytically.

Learn faster than your competitors

Arie de Geus says, 'the only way to preserve the competitive edge of your company is to make sure that your company **learns faster** than competitors.' Arie de Geus worked for Shell for 38 years in different jobs on three continents. Today he is an elegantly grizzled pensioner who tours the world lecturing at different conferences, charming in person and in thought. In the early 1980s he worked as co-ordinator of the worldwide planning unit of Shell. He used the job to demonstrate the connection between strategic planning and organisational learning. It was a lesson that earned him recognition as one of the pioneers of the learning organisation and he has inspired many people to develop learning organisations.

Learning is a precondition of the competitiveness of today's organisations surviving in the turmoil of continuous change. Today's organisations are, however, often very short-lived. Companies are established and dissolved with alarming speed. The operating life of even big enterprises is normally very short. In his book *The Living Company* (1997) Arie de Geus argued that the average operating life of an enterprise is much shorter than its potential. He claimed that enterprises died because their directors only concentrated on producing products and services and making money, and ignored the organisation as a society comprised of people working to survive.

Arie de Geus says that long-lived, **living enterprises** have a nature that makes wide ranging development possible. 'They know who they are; they understand what is their place in the world; they take care of their financial matters in the way that they have the possibility to control their future. These characteristics are reflected in operational models that enterprises use for their reorganisation in the course of generations. Living enterprises produce products and services in order to make their living in the same way as most of us work in order to be able to live.' Living enterprises value people more than property. They know that property is just a way to earn your living. 'For them, property and profits are like oxygen; important for life, but not the meaning of life.'

That's one way of looking at an enterprise – as a living organism. But we can also conceive of it as a machine, looking at it only as a tool for making money. But an organisation as a living organism is a systematic and comprehensive model in which the organisation is viewed as a place with a more permanent meaning. It is a more humane business entity providing people with the chance to make their living and implement their ideas. And in the future, successful long-lived organisations will be built on the model of a living enterprise in which learning and renewal is not just a short-term competitive factor, but a precondition for survival.

Nokia – an organisation under continuous renewal

Nokia is a good example of a Finnish enterprise that has endured a continuous restructuring process and survived. Founded in Tampere in **1865**, Nokia turned 135 in 2000. The founder was a Finnish mining engineer called **Fredrik Idestam**. In its early years, Nokia manufactured chip and sawn timber, paper and chemical pulp, and produced electricity. Later when the Finnish Rubber Factory (founded in 1898 in Helsinki) became involved in the operations the product selection extended to include galoshes, rubber boots and car and bicycle tyres. The Cable Factory of Finland, which was to become one of the pillars of Nokia, was founded in 1912, specialising in producing wires as well as telephone and electric cables.

Nokia's operations were reorganised in **1966**, when **Nokia Ltd., the Finnish Rubber Factory and the Cable Factory of Finland merged**. After the merger the cable business became the most important branch of the company. **The small electronics department of the cable unit grew fast into a branch of its own.** And over time, various new departments evolved, like the **telecommunications, IT, industrial automation and consumer electronics enterprises.** By **the 1970s Nokia had grown into a major business.** It had flourished into a multi-trade enterprise producing all kinds of things, from babies' nappies, to controlling systems for nuclear power plants.

In the 1980s, many branches of Nokia started to look abroad for new growth opportunities. This was particularly the case with Nokia Electronics. It was the company's strategy to become a European technology enterprise. Nokia's mobile phones, telecommunications network products, televisions and computers were quick to gain a foothold in Europe. By the end of the 1980s the share of electronics of the larger company's net sales had ballooned to 60 percent. And in the 1990s Nokia's business operations expanded to cover the whole world. It was at that point that the company determined to focus on its core areas and began to ditch most of the branches that had nothing to do with telecommunications. At the start of the new millennium, Nokia has become purely a global telecommunications company. Figure 1.2 shows Nokia's reorganisation process over the last few decades.

Nokia's success in the second half of the 1990s was phenomenal. Year after year, it improved on its results and watched its market value swell. The basis for this success was deeply rooted in the firm's history and there is no question that continuous learning and renewal played a vital role. Look at some of the language used to describe the global telecommunications business in recent years (Kulkki and Kosonen 1999):

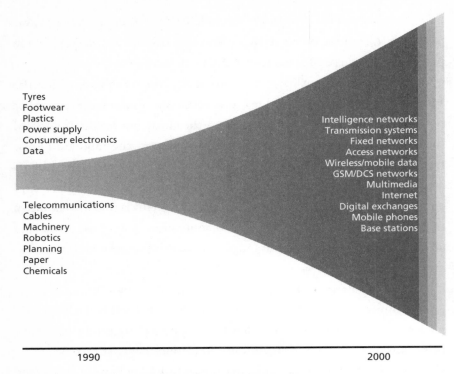

Tyres
Footwear
Plastics
Power supply
Consumer electronics
Data

Intelligence networks
Transmission systems
Fixed networks
Access networks
Wireless/mobile data
GSM/DCS networks
Multimedia
Internet

Telecommunications
Cables
Machinery
Robotics
Planning
Paper
Chemicals

Digital exchanges
Mobile phones
Base stations

1990   2000

Fig. 1.2   Nokia's reorganisation process from a multi-trade company to a
telecommunications company

- fast growth and turbulence;
- tough competition and, simultaneously, cooperation between competitors;
- active exploitation of new business possibilities (markets creating strategy);
- very short product life cycle;
- strong standardisation and technology-based competition;
- the importance of right timing; and
- the speed in bringing new innovations to the markets.

Operating in a market like this requires adjusting and stretching as well as continuous learning on the level of the individual, the team and the organisation.

Nokia started its progress towards becoming a global telecommunications company in 1992 under the direction of Jorma Ollila. At the time Nokia's strategic ambition was expressed by four themes – global, focus, telecommunications and value added. This new approach was quickly absorbed by staff and clearly became the driving force of the firm. Nokia succeeded extremely well in its quick transformation and globalisation process. All of it was achieved with the help of the young, ambitious and technically competent, but inexperienced personnel that was given a lot of responsibility and plenty of challenge.

But it helped determine Nokia's present mode of operations and its emphasis on respect for individuals and customers, a sharp focus on customer and employee satisfaction, and continuous learning underpinned by a strong desire for achievement. And these were values that made Nokia one of the quickest learning organisations in the world.

In 1999 Nokia's turnover was 19,772 million Euros, annual growth of a stunning 48%. The market value of the capital stock was 209,371 million Euros, annual growth of 250%. At the end of 1999 Nokia employed 55,260 persons.

What is learning?

Learning can be defined in a lot of ways. It is change, development, growth and maturation. It is a continuous process. Part of it is target-oriented and planned activity, but part of it is incidental and unexpected. Learning is selective – new information is filtered through previous experiences. In general, it requires time for **reflection** and evaluation. Unique experiences (those of the individual, team and organisation) are analysed and evaluated as part of the learning process. They are compared to previous experiences and attached to wider frames of reference. And all this leads to the creation of an operation model that can be applied in the future.

The definition of learning

Let's define learning like this:

Learning is a process in which the individual gathers new knowledge, skills, attitudes, experiences and contacts that produce changes in his/her behaviour.

This definition includes the following essential points:

- Learning is a process influenced by cognitive (intellectual), affective (emotional) and psychomotor areas.
- An individual interpretation is always generated by the acquisition of knowledge or other targets of learning. Learning is not mechanical, but creates meaning through experiences.
- Learning is not only gathering knowledge – skills, attitudes and feelings as well as values are at least as important as new knowledge. Very often the role of information is over-emphasised in learning. It is a major part of learning but is by no means the full extent of the process.
- All kinds of experiences, both new ones and old, are important. The more prior experience we have, the easier it is for us to learn from the new experiences. Indeed, many things require sufficient experience of life – different jobs – before we can really understand them.
- The meaning of contacts should be obvious in everyday learning. Very often the quickest way to learn, to get information on various matters, is through a wide and working contact network.
- True learning involves application and this, in general, means that something changes through learning; operational models and ways of thinking are changed by learning. And these changes can occur on the level of thinking, feelings or behaviour.

Staircase of learning

Learning can take place on many levels (see Fig. 1.3). But before we even start talking about knowing, it is worth acknowledging the significance of recognising when we don't know something. The realisation of one's own ignorance is in some respects a precondition for learning something new.

The primary level of knowing relates to the acquisition of knowledge. All too often, traditional school learning remains on this level. Moving up the staircase, understanding means that the learnt material has really been absorbed. It affects the attitudes and feelings of the individual. Understanding generally requires a considerably longer period of reflection than just knowing or remembering. The next step, application, means that we can really apply what we have learnt and implement it successfully. It means mastering the levels of knowing and understanding. Finally, there is the level of development, which means reorganising our already mastered action models. True learning includes all levels.

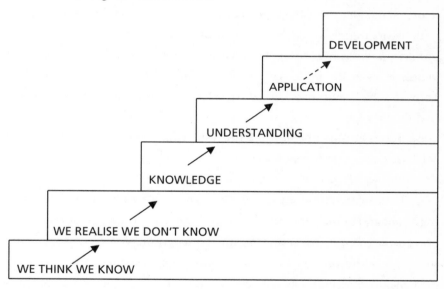

Fig. 1.3 Staircase of learning

Types of learning

There are four different types of learning; reactive learning, predictive learning, action learning and transformative learning. They do not necessarily eliminate one another, and can comfortably coexist. **Reactive learning** means that the individual or organisation learns from experience and the evaluation of experience. We face a certain situation to which we react in a certain manner, producing a given result. After this we evaluate our working methods and our results and make conclusions on how to operate in the future. This probably affects our thinking and method of working.

Predictive learning means that we try to foresee the future so that we can choose a better working method. We start by thinking how events will unfold so that we can come up with a plan of future action. We implement the plan, see how it fits the eventual situation and then assess its effectiveness. This evaluation ultimately produces a form of learning.

The third type of learning is **action learning**. Action learning is a type of learning described for the first time by Reg Revans who is one of the foremost thinkers about the concept of the learning organisation. He first articulated the idea more than 50 years ago and further elaborated his theory in the years that followed. Revans says there is no learning without action nor action without learning. It starts with a practical problem. A group of people assesses the underlying problem, thinks about what they need to know to solve it and comes up with a solution. The group can be composed of different types of people who are not very familiar with the problem situation. It can be implemented and the result can then be evaluated. We split action learning into two sub-sectors – firstly, when the group comes up with its solution and secondly, when it is applied.

The fourth type of learning is **transformative learning**. It means taking a root and branch approach to analysing events, asking questions about every aspect of why we do what we do. It often means completely overhauling our thought processes and can produce major change. A typical decision-making process is based on corrective measures dictated by present action models. So-called single-loop learning will only correct measures in the framework of the existing action model. But double-loop learning takes place when the evaluation process is not aimed at the action itself, but at the underlying action model. From time to time we should challenge our action models and change them where necessary.

Today's turbulent environment emphasises predictive and transformative learning. We must continuously question old action models and look for new ones. All learning demands time for reflection, something we would do well to remember in the middle of all this rush. Predictive and transformative learning, which produce more complex solutions, are more time consuming.

During the last few years I have experienced myself that I don't have enough time for learning and renewal. I had the feeling that I lose track of a lot of things. It's probably a feeling familiar to many of us today. The technological development of the telecommunications industry suffers the turmoil of constant change. There is no time for professional renewal and self-development. The exploitation of the Internet and different kinds of computer software doesn't solve the problem. We feel that we should know much more.

My normal daily routine didn't afford me the time to narrow my competence gap so I decided to realise my long-time dream of a sabbatical year. I spent most of the time in reflecting, analysing and understanding certain things. For me this was predictive and transformative learning in practice. And I firmly believe that the need for this type of sabbatical and self-development break will become more and more common in the future.

The learning process

Because learning is such an important process, we should understand how the learning process takes place and how different people learn. There are distinct efficiency benefits from getting to grips with the learning process and its different styles. Perhaps the most famous basic model of the learning process is the Kolb model that I will describe here. It says that learning is a process in which knowledge is created by transforming experiences. It is closely connected to practical experiences and it is assumed that the learner already has some work or other similar experience that allows him to evaluate his own activity. It is also crucial that he has the motivation to develop himself because motivation – desire to learn – is the starting point of all learning. Without that, learning is not really possible. The Kolb model does a good job of describing the learning process of an adult. Figure 1.4 shows the basic model of the learning process.

Everything starts from **experiences** and from the fact that we have the desire to learn from our experiences. The desire to learn, a certain kind of

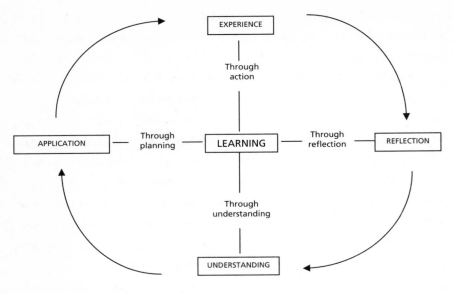

Fig. 1.4   The basic model of the learning process

curiosity, wondering, is raw material for learning. We should also have time for **reflection;** time to deliberate and possibly to acquire knowledge connected to the experience. Different views and facts are then processed and transformed into knowledge which, again, we should comprehend and **understand.** At this phase we normally have a sort of 'aha' experience and feel clearly that we now understand this. Everyone who has proceeded from the level of knowing to the level of understanding, knows how big a difference there is between the two.

Learning through experiences also includes an abstract conceptualisation. The thinking process regenerates knowledge that will be used in the interpretation of the experience. The next phase is **application**. Knowledge that has been fully understood and absorbed is put into practice and experimented with in different contexts. Knowledge can expand and deepen in the application phase.

It is vital to understand that the learning process includes all these phases. We learn both by doing and understanding, and through the acquisition and expansion of knowledge. We get experience through doing things and during the evaluation phase that experience is transformed into knowledge. That knowledge will be processed later during the understanding phase. And in the application phase this knowledge is further expanded. The learning process should be planned so that it covers all phases.

On top of all that, there are four factors which support the learning process. Firstly we need a desire to learn new things, i.e. a learning motivation. Secondly, we need some intuitive understanding, internal success, experience of understanding something. Thirdly, we have an ambition to experiment and, fourthly, it is beneficial to 'document' the learning process somehow. This means that we memorise the things learnt, write them down or save them in some database. This is how we make sure that we are able to implement the things learnt when we run into the same kind of experience the next time. These factors are presented in Fig. 1.5.

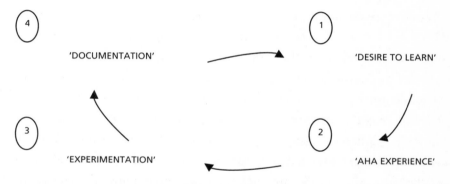

Fig. 1.5 Factors supporting the learning process

It is very important also to understand that learning is not a mechanical process but a very complex creative process. Previous experiences and attitudes have an essential impact on learning. It is not just about collecting new information, because all our observations are filtered through old experiences. Sometimes previous experiences and attitudes can be the biggest obstacles to learning. Figure 1.6 shows how previous experiences affect the learning process.

We all look at the world with our own particular set of spectacles. We build an analytical framework out of our thought processes and unique set of references, all of which have a major impact on our activities and the

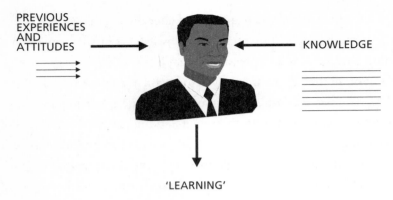

PREVIOUS EXPERIENCES AND ATTITUDES → ← **KNOWLEDGE**

↓

'LEARNING'

Fig. 1.6   Dependency of learning on previous experiences

way we learn. We have been programmed with images since birth and this programming goes on all the time, although we are not always aware of it. Very often we remain prisoners of our own, old, negative images. We must, however, be able to free ourselves from these images and create new, positive, constructive ones in their place.

Learning and all our observations are always interpreted individually. That interpretation is born out of our own experiences. And it explains why different people experience the same things very differently. William James, one of the pioneers in psychology, said, 'A man is the only creature who can change his living conditions by changing his own attitudes.' G. W. Allport, social psychologist, expressed the same idea by saying, 'The attitudes of the individual determine what he sees and hears, what he thinks and what he does.' This idea of individual interpretation should be kept in mind through life in general. For a long time, Eastern philosophy has taught that events themselves do not break people. It is the way they react to these events that can break them.

Individual learning styles

Kolb's model of the learning process has provided a starting point for many of the models that have been built to describe different learning styles. Peter Honey and Alan Mumford developed one of these styles. It divides people into four basic types – activist, reflector, theorist and pragmatist. Figure 1.7 presents these learning styles.

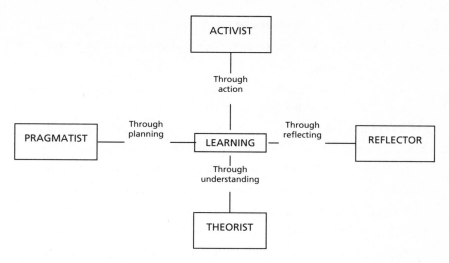

Fig. 1.7 Different kinds of learning styles

The activist learns best through activity. He does not respond well to theoretical exercises, but looks for practical solutions. **The reflector** learns best when he can collect and evaluate new information in peace. He likes to follow things from a distance, and analyses what others are doing. For him learning must be a methodical process and he finds it difficult to adapt to rapid change.

The theorist learns best by reasoning and by building logical models. He wants to ask questions, experiment and analyse the matter from different angles. He must really get to grips with the issues before he is satisfied, and is a model of thoroughness. **The pragmatist** learns best by experimenting. He learns when confronting tough problems and when involved in a lot of action. He does not generally bother to get acquainted with matters very deeply, but prefers to respond quickly.

The identification of one's own learning style helps in the evaluation of where and how we learn best. It also helps us to develop a learning style that differs from our normal, but we need to go through the whole learning process in order to learn effectively, and we need to master all learning styles. We develop our learning skills by exploiting all the different styles; by implementing, deliberating, thinking and participating. Think about your own basic learning style. Are there other styles you could use? How can you develop your style selection and how can you learn together with people using different styles? A general description of these styles is presented below.

Activists

Activists involve themselves fully and without bias in new experiences. They enjoy the here and now and are happy to be dominated by immediate experiences. They are open-minded, not sceptical and this tends to make them enthusiastic about anything new. Their philosophy is: 'I will try anything once'. They tend to act first and consider the consequences afterwards. Their days are filled with activity. They tackle problems by brainstorming. As soon as the excitement from one activity has died down they are busy looking for the next. They tend to thrive on the challenge of new experiences but are bored with the implementation and long-term consolidation. They are gregarious people constantly involving themselves with others but, in doing so, seeking to centre all activities around themselves.

Reflectors

Reflectors like to stand back to ponder upon experiences and observe them from many different perpectives. They collect data, both first hand and from others, and prefer to think about it thoroughly before coming to any conclusion. The thorough collection and analysis of data about experiences and events is what counts so they tend to postpone drawing definite conclusions as long as possible. Their philosphy is to be cautious. They are thoughtful people who like to consider all possible angles and implications before making a move. They prefer to take a back seat in meetings and discussions. They enjoy observing other people in action. They listen to others and get the drift of the discussion before making their own points. They tend to adopt a low profile and have a slightly distant, tolerant, unruffled air about them. Their reaction will be a part of a wider figure including the past as well as the present and other people's observations as well as their own.

Theorists

Theorists adapt and integrate observations into complex but logically sound theories. They think problems through in a vertical, step by step, logical way. They assimilate disparate facts into coherent theories. They tend to be perfectionists who won't rest easy until things are tidy and fit into a rational scheme. They like to analyse and synthesise. They are keen on basic assumptions, principles, theories, models and system thinking. Their philosophy rewards rationality and logic. 'If it is logical, it is good.' Questions they frequently ask are: 'Does it make sense? How does this fit with that? What are the basic assumptions?' They tend to be detached, analytical and dedicated to rational objectivity rather than anything subjective or ambiguous. Their approach to problems is consistently logical. This is their 'mental set' and they rigidly reject anything that doesn't fit with it. They prefer to maximise certainty and feel uncomfortable with subjective judgements, lateral thinking and anything flippant.

Pragmatists

Pragmatists are keen on trying out ideas, theories and techniques to see if they work in practice. They positively search out new ideas and take the first opportunity to experiment with applications. They are the sort of people who return from management courses brimming with new ideas that they want to try out in practice. They like to get on with things and act quickly and confidently on ideas that attract them. They tend to be impatient with ruminating and open-ended discussions. They are essentialy practical, down to earth people who like making practical decisions and solving problems. They respond to problems and opportunities 'as a challenge'. Their philosophy is: 'There is always a better way' and 'If it works, it's good'.

Honey and Mumford, 1986

Obstacles of learning

The obstacles of learning are related to the different phases of the learning process. They can also be examined separately from the viewpoint of the individual, the team or the whole organisation. The following obstacles are linked to learning through action:

- there is no desire to learn, motivation is low and there are no clear learning targets;
- the scope of observation is narrow and the individual is overspecialised; and
- there is no sensitivity to picking up weak signals or the individual is too 'thick-skinned'.

Obstacles of knowledge collection and reflection are:

- lack of time;
- there is no information available;
- information is conflicting, inconsistent or ambiguous;
- there is too much information; and
- insufficient 'documentation'; experience is not documented and cannot be remembered or shared.

The following obstacles are related to learning through understanding:

- there is no time for reflection, evaluation of matters;
- understanding is not considered necessary, superficial knowledge is considered to be enough;
- conclusions are in conflict with previous knowledge; and
- there is too big a difference between existing and new data.

The following obstacles are linked to application:

- things are forgotten, if documentation is insufficient;
- there is no scope to experiment;
- application is not supported; and
- things are not carried through; lack of long-term planning.

Obviously, by eliminating these obstacles we can intensify and improve learning considerably. And that means creating a favourable environment for learning in the organisation. Bert Juch identified the key obstacles to learning when he developed his model and they have subsequently been described by Kari Lahti in a particularly evocative form:

- small window that restricts the amount of observations;
- thick skin that restricts the reception of observations;
- closed gate that prevents the implementation of plans; and
- wide river that prevents the completion of plans.

We might look at things from too small a window. Our viewpoint is too limited and we are really only interested in a few things. We do not actively collect data nor observe our environment in a wider sense. Neither do we pay attention to the feelings of other people.

Too thick a skin is about being impermeable. New thoughts cannot come through. We do not want to listen to the opinions of others, particularly if we disagree with them. Nor do we approve of or want to listen to criticism directed to us. We are overspecialised and it is difficult for us to accept new points of view.

Closed or narrow gate means that it is difficult to start new things. We hesitate and hang back when we should start something new. We want to be sure that we succeed before we try new things. We are preoccupied with the fear of failure.

Wide river means that things are often left unfinished. Difficulties and problems tend to discourage us. When we try to cross the stream we often notice that it is too wide and we turn back.

These obstacles all disturb the learning process. So we should identify our own obstacles to learning and try to look at the world out of a somewhat bigger window, be more sensitive in adopting new things, open our gate wide open and try new working methods, even allowing for some risks. We should also be able to cross the wide river and finish the things we have started. When running into difficulties and problems we should try even harder. We should always be able to challenge assumptions and see things from a different viewpoint. To quote the French novelist Marcel Proust: 'The real wonder of finding new things is not in looking for new views, but in looking at things with new eyes.' We set our own limits and that means the limits of what we can learn.

For teams, the biggest obstacles of learning are:

- knowledge and competence is not shared in a team;
- lack of common targets;
- lack of common language and readiness to discuss;
- poor human relations and poor interaction skills; and
- ambiguous methods.

Many obstacles to learning can also be demonstrated on the level of the organisation. They can be called the organisation's learning disturbances and are as follows:

- amnesia (lack of organisational memory or memory that works inefficiently);
- superstition (biased interpretation of reality);
- schizophrenia (lack of coordination between the different parts of the organisation);
- learnt helplessness (the members of the organisation do not believe that things can be changed);
- paralysis (inability to act);
- tunnel vision (very one-sided view of things);
- information block (information is withheld);
- mania (plenty of unplanned activity, nobody knows where it is going to lead);
- burnout (the organisation is getting tired and cannot implement a new reorganisation process); and
- inflammation (personnel relations are so badly tangled that reasonable activity is no longer possible).

Consider what kind of learning disabilities there are in your organisation.

Level of learning

We have already discussed how learning takes place on an individual, a team and an organisational level. And it is crucial that learning is supported on all these levels. More often than not, too little attention has been paid to learning in general. Only lately have we started to understand what kind of benefits there are in intensifying learning. We know that an individual uses only 1–10% of his brain capacity. We could speculate that the organisation also uses only about 10% of its know-how potential. And that must mean organisational, team and individual learning can be intensified enormously.

We can for example:

- make continuous learning one of the basic values of the organisation;
- create a working environment that genuinely supports learning;
- organise 'how to learn' courses;
- develop concrete models for learning at work;
- establish learning centres in the different parts of the organisation; and
- develop virtual learning methods (computer-aided education, net education etc.).

Figure 1.8 shows the connection of individual, team and organisational learning. Good contact networks are important both inside and between the different levels. Individuals create their own opportunity to learn continuously by questioning and actively developing their own operations. Sharing competencies and learning together is the benefit of working in teams. But it's the common vision and values of the organisation that control the learning process. The organisation puts together the teams and individuals by giving them challenges. The organisation also creates the structures supporting learning and rewards the development of competence.

In this model, the teams are the intermediators. The team becomes the basic unit of learning in which the competence of the individuals and the competence of the team are transformed into organisational competence that can benefit other teams.

Sharing competencies inside the team and between other teams is crucial. It is also important to have sufficient contacts with outsiders on an individual and a team level. This kind of learning in a team requires good interaction skills; we have to know how to play together. A lone top performer can be useless to an organisation if he/she does not have enough contacts. He/she is driven into a corner and cut off from the outside world.

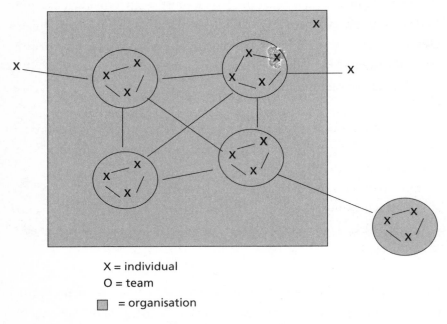

X = individual
O = team
⬛ = organisation

Fig. 1.8 Organisational, team and individual learning

Individual learning

Individual learning is, of course, the starting point of all learning. All learning takes place on an individual level at first. Learning is a process in which the individual collects knowledge, skills, attitudes, experiences and contacts that lead into changes in his behaviour. Learning should be seen as a skill that can be developed. Learning skill (studying skill) consists of the following factors: studying attitudes, studying methods and techniques (note-making, memorising and reading technique). The general intelligence level of the person in question and any earlier knowledge he might have on the subject have, of course, an impact on the process of learning. According to researchers the learning skills can easily be improved as much as 10–50% by developing these elements of learning. Tony Buzan and Edward de Bono have published several useful books on this subject.

I have described the individual learning cycle as follows (see Fig. 1.9). Learning is a process in which experiences are turned to competence. Individual experiences are evaluated and information collected from these experiences. After this the aim is to comprehend and understand the knowledge. Then follows the application phase when the knowledge will be put into practice and used in different connections. A perfect learning process

Fig. 1.9 Individual learning cycle

includes all these phases.

Team learning

Organisations are increasingly operating on a team level. The ambition of the team is to form a small group of people whose competencies complement each other. It is committed to a common objective, common performance targets and common action model. And the team feels common responsibility for its performance (so said Katzenbauch and Smith 1994).

Team learning, from an organisational perspective, is as important as individual learning. And as with individual learning, we will define team learning as a process in which the team acquires knowledge, skills, attitudes, experiences and contacts that lead to changes in the behaviour of the team.

The learning cycle of the team can be described as follows (see Fig. 1.10). The starting point is the current operation of the team. The team should regularly evaluate its own operations so it can improve its performance and agree targets for the future

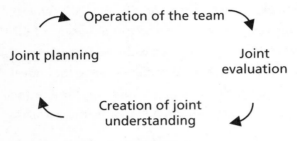

Fig. 1.10 The learning cycle of the team

The preconditions of team learning are that the team has common targets and action models and shared responsibility. Good team spirit is also vitally important. The team must have a joint language and readiness to discuss. Sharing knowledge and competence is also important. Basically, team learning means the team members can work well together and can effectively exploit their individual competencies. The aim is that the collective competence is greater than the sum of its individual parts. In a sense it is a combination of individual and organisational learning. Senge argues that the team learning process is made up of the following components:

- Evaluation of experiences takes place in a team.
- Common understanding, vision and values as well as an internal model, steer joint thinking patterns and activity.
- Measures are planned together and it is decided what is to be implemented and how, who is doing what, when and how. The plan also includes the analysis of what kind of competence is needed and at what stage, how this competence is acquired and who is responsible for managing the learning process.
- Each member can implement his own share of actual operations, even in the absence of other members. The development of the joint thinking

model and the drafting of the action plan provide such a solid base for the operations of the team that the final result of learning, even if implemented in many separate measures, will conform to the common objectives.

Organisational learning

Can the organisation learn? The answer depends on how we define the organisation and learning. As we explored earlier, the organisation can be viewed as a mechanical model or as a living organism model. An organisation can learn just like individuals and teams, if it behaves like a living organism and not a machine-like functional organisation. Living organisms are open systems interacting with their environment. They have the ability to handle knowledge and learn, learn how to learn better, establish contacts, and to reorganise their own operations continuously. At present, there is a clear trend towards the living organism organisation model. And the future learning organisations will be connected and virtual organisations, in which some of the traditional limits to learning have disappeared. Speed of renewal will be a defining feature of these future organisations.

Organisational learning can be defined as the **ability of the organisation to renew and change its operations.** In practice renewal means the organisation is ready to continuously look for new competence areas either connected to the company's core business or other operations linked with the working methods, processes and guidelines of the organisation. Perhaps the most typical processes supporting renewal are the strategy, knowledge, competence and performance management processes.

Organisational learning can also be described as a learning cycle. The starting point is the organisation's operations out of which versatile feedback is systematically collected. The feedback produces information that is interpreted in co-operation And these interpretations provide material to help determine the company's vision, strategy and objectives. This is, to an extent, how the thinking and action models and competence of the organisation are developed. In organisational learning the feedback culture and systems play a key role. And it's also important to appreciate the part played by strategic learning – the ability of the management and the entire staff to read weak signals and renew their structures accordingly.

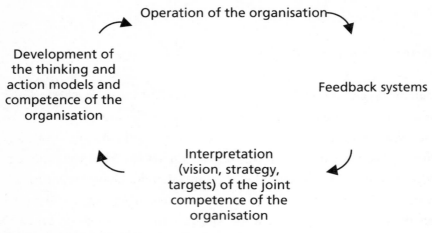

Fig. 1.11   The learning cycle of the organisation

Organisational learning differs from individual and team learning but there are similar themes (Marquardt 1996). Firstly, it occurs, through shared perception, competence and thinking models. Secondly, it is based on previous knowledge and experience as defined by the memory of the organisation embodied in its working methods, processes and regulations. Although individual and team learning and organisational learning are closely connected, organisational learning is not simply the sum of individual and team learning.

Learning skills of the organisation

A learning organisation versus organisational learning

The concept of a learning organisation has been discussed a lot recently. Below I have listed some well-known definitions of the learning organisation but my own definition of it is simply the following:

A learning organisation has the ability to continuously adjust to new situations, to change and to renew itself according to the demands of the environment. It learns from experience and can quickly change its ways of working.

All organisations are learning organisations but some learn faster than others. They would all like to be the fastest but continuously repeat the same mistakes. Making mistakes is fine – indeed mistakes are all part of the true learning process – but we have to ensure we learn from our mistakes.

Learning is really the core of the business in a learning organisation, but it is also vital to be able to implement the rapid changes in the ways we work that are prescribed by the learning process. Immediate implementation, application and further development of what we have learnt is at the heart of the effective learning organisation.

Having said all that, the term learning organisation is not really very good because all organisations learn to greater or lesser extents. I prefer to use the term intelligent organisation. An intelligent organisation has three basic abilities as part of its powers of renewal:

- it sees the need for change at a very early stage;
- it learns faster than its competitors; and
- it can implement new things faster than its competitors.

And going even further, the operation model of an intelligent organisation can be described as follows:

- it learns fast and renews itself continuously;
- it supports continuous learning and improvement of performance of individuals and teams;
- it has a distinct vision and values steering its operations;
- it allows mistakes and learns from them;
- it takes good care of the competence, commitment and wellbeing of its employees;

- it relates closely with the customer and takes good care of customer satisfaction; and
- it always operates according to the principles of sustainable development.

Ultimately it is more productive to talk about organisational learning than about learning organisations. Organisational learning is something more concrete. And we should make it ever more concrete by describing different models. I have defined organisational learning as follows:

> *Organisational learning means that the organisation is able to renew itself by changing its working methods, processes and values. In practice, renewal means that the organisation is ready to acquire new competence and exploit that competence immediately.*

Just as we support other forms of learning with different processes, so we should support organisational learning. That means things like performance, competence and knowledge management. We should also create a favourable environment for learning.

The organisation's ten most important learning skills

According to Peter Senge (1990) an effective learning organisation continuously develops its ability to create its own future. It learns faster than its competitors. People create their reality, realise it and are empowered by it. The key question here is about making sense of the knowledge and knowing how to apply it, not just about receiving knowledge mechanically. In his book *The Fifth Discipline* Senge lists five components of a learning organisation; system thinking, self-control, internal action models, common vision and team learning. Michael Marquardt (1996) added a sixth skill in the form of dialogue.

I would like to add strategic learning, feedback systems, data systems and sharing of knowledge. That produces a list of ten items that represent the organisation's most important skills supporting learning. They are skills that can be developed and should be actively targeted, if we want to support organisational learning. Success at the organisational level depends on

Definitions of a learning organisation

A learning organisation is an organisation where people have the possibility of developing themselves continuously and achieving the results they want, where new thinking models are born, where people have common targets and where people learn together.

Senge, 1991

A learning enterprise is an organisation helping every member to learn and renew itself and its environment consciously.

Pedler, Burgoyne ja Boydell, 1997

A learning organisation is an organisation where the members of the organisation question the operations continuously, find mistakes or differences and fix these themselves by restructuring their organisation and operations.

Argyris, 1993

A learning organisation is an organisation creating, acquiring and transferring competence and being able to change its behaviour according to new knowledge and views.

Garwin, 1993

A learning organisation is an organisation urging people to try, allowing mistakes and failure, encouraging internal competition, increasing and transmitting knowledge and promoting innovation.

Peters, 1993

A learning organisation is an organisation that learns and encourages people to learn.

Handy, 1991

how everyday working practice incorporates these skills. To summarise, the organisation's most important learning skills are:

1   System thinking
2   Mental models steering operations
3   Strategic learning
4   Use of feedback systems
5   Self-management
6   Team learning
7   Dialogue
8   Shared vision
9   Exploitation of information systems
10 Sharing competence and knowledge

System thinking is about identifying the interaction between different entities within the organisation. We are used to seeing things linearly from a
stable perspective. But reality does not consist of linear relations only, but of
processes connected to each other and influencing each other. System thinking recognises that everything affects everything else. Changing one thing
might influence many other things. We must learn to perceive complex entities.

    Mental models guide our operations and we have to be sure to under-
stand how they affect our decision-making. They determine how we see the
world and how we act in certain situations. They are often unconscious and
embedded deep in our routine. The shared framework of the organisation is
created on the basis of these models and includes the organisation's culture
and values. From time to time, they need to be analysed to make sure they
really do enable effective renewal and support the long-term ambitions and
abilities of the organisation.

    Strategic learning means the ability of the management – and more
and more often the whole staff – to interpret the world, question thinking
models and identify new ones. It means checking that the organisation's
strategy is appropriately founded and able to respond quickly to change. We
must react fast to the evolving needs of the customers and the changes to
the competitive environment. We must read weak signals from the market
place. Strategic learning helps us in checking our direction fast, while opera-

tive learning helps us in creating new competence and working methods that meet the demands of a new direction.

Traditional strategic views based on price and costs and specialisation no longer guarantee competitive edge. Competence-based strategies are commonplace now in many organisations. Fast renewal is a must and competence and learning as well as the readiness to make prompt changes are the key factors in competition.

Building **feedback systems** is a crucial skill in an organisation. They must be built on an individual, a team and an organisational level. Giving and receiving well-timed feedback can prevent problems or at least offer the right sort of solution for many problems. Feedback is also a precondition for growth and development. It needs to come from all directions. The implementation of feedback systems generally demands a certain type of culture characterised by open and direct communication.

Self-management (personal mastery) is a typical feature of an intelligent organisation. It means that individuals can influence their own development and learning. Organisational structure becomes flatter and hierarchies are shrunk and individuals are expected to work independently. Management is delegated to units and teams. It is important in self-management to concentrate on the essentials and analyse the situation clearly. Other important characteristics are a strong commitment to work, initiative, a sense of responsibility, recognition of one's own development targets and continuous development. Organisations are all too often pretty poor at making full use of their employees' energies and mental capacity.

Team learning is another key part of an intelligent organisation. Individual learning is important, but does not go far enough to fertilise organisational learning. It is team learning that helps us find insights that individuals would not have found by themselves. Teams are the basic units of learning. Efficient team work is a prerequisite of success in knowledge-intensive enterprises.

A shared vision makes sure we are going in the same direction. It needs an emotional component and should be subscribed to at every level of the organisation. Without that clarity of vision, the organisation is limited in the extent to which it can develop competencies. Creating a common vision and communicating this vision to the whole organisation is a vital skill in an effective intelligent organisation.

There should also be plenty of **active dialogue** in an intelligent organisation. That means deliberating on different questions and problems, listening attentively to other people's thoughts and questioning one's own thoughts. In a dialogue, people express different views and are required to defend them. The aim is to find the best possible solution together. Dialogue helps us to see new possibilities and assists the organisation in the learning process. A true dialogue requires an open organisational culture that allows, even encourages, questions and differences of opinion.

Developing **information systems** and knowing how to use them plays a major role in organisational learning. Information systems form an integral part of the competence of the organisation. Data systems have traditionally had an implementing role, but are, today, more important in an enabling role. Information systems make totally new working methods possible and provide innovative solutions. Electronic trading is a good example of this kind of change.

These are all very well as means of enhancing organisational learning but they can all too easily come to nothing without one crucial ingredient. **Sharing**. It is sharing knowledge and competence that generates the real power. It is not necessarily altogether straightforward and at the very least demands plenty of trust if information is to flow smoothly through the organisation. But a collective belief that everyone stands to benefit from sharing knowledge can unlock a great deal of power within the organisation.

Learning and feedback

Feedback is another of the cornerstones of learning. Feedback is valuable for individual, team and organisational learning. But we have not yet built enough different feedback systems to support learning. We need to pay much more attention to the role of feedback in the workplace. Continuous and well-timed feedback prevents all sorts of problems. Couple that with a reciprocal openness to receiving feedback and you have the bedrock of all sorts of learning and growth.

The meaning of feedback for the individual

Here's a situation that will be familiar to lots of HR managers. It's a drama that plays itself over and over again in all sorts of workplaces. I've certainly come across it on a number of occasions. Let's call it the case of John Doe. John's superior asks for an appointment in order to tell the HR manager that John is a 'hopeless' case who has to be fired immediately. The boss insists it's been going on for years and is irredeemable. The HR manager replies by agreeing that it's a hopeless case – assuming, of course, that John has been made aware of the gravity of the situation and has received plenty of feedback. 'You've had regular development discussions with him, I'm sure?' says the HR manager. The boss answers by complaining that he does not understand anything and does not accept feedback. 'During the last few years there has been no point having development discussions with him.'

When we take a closer look at the players in this drama we will almost always find the same formula. John is a quiet, middle-aged professional who has been doing the same job for the last ten years and has, in a way, been excluded and become passive. He's unhappy with the coaching, training and feedback he has received and he is unhappy with his boss.

And the boss – he's invariably busy and impatient. He likes to take care of things left undone by his subordinates. He expects top results from them, but has problems coaching them and giving feedback. He just expects everybody to work independently.

In a way John is partly to blame for his own exclusion. But so is his superior, who has waited too long for things to get better. If the situation carries on unaddressed for long enough, the personal relations become entangled and it is extremely difficult to do anything. One can only ask why nothing was done before, why feedback was not given by both parties, why no development discussions were organised. Both parties are responsible for steering themselves down this cul-de-sac.

Our reenactment of John's drama may have been a little simplistic but the same narrative recurs all too often. Because the role of feedback at the workplace is so important, we should pay more attention to the development of feedback systems and feedback culture on an individual, a team and an organisational level.

The difficulty of giving feedback

Why do we feel that giving, and sometimes also receiving, feedback is so difficult? Why do we discover that the lack of feedback is so often a big problem in the workplace? On an individual level, it is often because so many people find giving feedback, particularly corrective feedback, a very hard thing to do and full of conflicting emotions. Communication culture in the workplace has traditionally been very flat – we do not easily reproach or praise other people. (This, of course, conflicts with our discovery that continuous development requires continuous feedback.)

Good interpersonal skills are crucial in a healthy organisation. We should know how to offer criticism tactfully, and how to give credit whenever possible. The Finnish ice hockey team is a good example of how this works in practice. Hannu Aravita, chief coach of the national side, said in a Nokia training session that he thought the difference between a good hockey team and the top team was tiny – but that critical difference was the accomplishment of the coach. And his primary tool was continuous feedback. Similarly, coaching in the workplace should be a continuous process of constructive dialogue between the superior and his or her subordinates. They should always be trying to improve their present and future performance by using systematic and versatile feedback.

The development of multiple feedback systems is frequently neglected in an organisation, which prefers to concentrate on the feedback it gets from its financial performance. It is like driving a car by looking only in the rear-view mirror. Fortunately, there are now top companies who have gone further lately – they've introduced steps to monitor feedback by measuring customer satisfaction, internal processes and the competence and satisfaction of the personnel.

Feedback systems of the organisation

An effective organisation has built different processes on different levels to gather feedback. Its feedback system consists of different kinds of tools that are used to extract feedback from individuals, teams and at the organisational level. The feedback system can be examined from the point of view of the feedback giver, the content of the feedback and the tools used. Also, the feedback receiver can be examined on three different levels: individual; team; and organisation. Figure 1.12 tabulates the different components of a typical feedback system. It can assimilate the information it accumulates from all the different constituent parts.

	FEEDBACK RECEIVER		
	INDIVIDUAL	TEAM	ORGANISATION
FEEDBACK GIVER	Employee Colleague Manager	Team member	Personnel Customers Owners Subcontractors Suppliers Training institutions Corporate image
FEEDBACK CONTENT	Performance Competence	Team efficiency, competence and satisfaction	Finance Stock exchange rates Quality/internal processes Satisfaction • personnel • customers Competence (human capital)
TOOLS	Free-form feedback Planning and development – discussions Assessment reports Leadership assessment 360-feedback tools	Team feedback • about the team • to members	Personnel surveys Customer satisfaction Surveys Induction surveys Exit interviews Quality audits Financial reports Corporate image study

Fig. 1.12   The feedback system of the organisation

Feedback should be given at every level. There should, for example, be a lot of emphasis on team feedback, if only because working in teams is becoming more and more common. Often the teams do not work very efficiently and blending into a truly effective team takes a surprisingly long time. The team needs to get regular and systematic feedback in order to improve its performance. And this kind of feedback is still more often the exception than the rule.

There is also a lot of effort these days directed at looking for feedback from as many sources as possible. We talk about 360-degree feedback. On an individual level that means feedback comes from the boss, subordinates, colleagues and possibly even from other business partners. On the enterprise level, we've seen the development and widespread adoption of ways of gauging customer satisfaction and employee satisfaction.

So how do we manage feedback? Planning and development discussions and employee surveys are the most commonly used tools. Few workplaces actively use any other tools. 360-degree feedback surveys, for example, are still relatively uncommon on a large scale. Some businesses have used them for a long time in leadership appraisals. But the 360-degree feedback systems have started to surface in the area of teamwork, customer service and evaluation of interpersonal skills.

Nokia uses all tools that are shown in Fig. 1.13. Yearly customer satisfaction and employee satisfaction studies are very important tools and team feedback is used more and more often. It helps in the systematic development of teamwork. Different kinds of 360-degree feedback surveys are also actively tested. The leadership and management skills of the superiors have been regularly evaluated for 15 years with the help of feedback from subordinates, colleagues and superiors. An anonymous survey is made at three-year intervals. Taken the right way, it is a great tool for improving one's own behaviour as a boss. The feedback is collected and interpreted by an external psychologist with whom you can discuss your own development areas uninhibitedly.

The importance of the feedback culture

If the enterprise has a working feedback system, it should support organisational learning. It enables the business to continuously renew its processes and invite challenges. But the implementation of these feedback systems demands a certain kind of culture and values. A good feedback culture needs openness, trust, respect for the individual, informative communication, an acceptance of mistakes, good team spirit, support for other people and an ambition for continuous learning. The feedback system does not work without all these values.

I got a good insight into an organisational culture when I was working at Nixdorf in Germany at the turn of the 1990s. That was the point at which the two German enterprises, Nixdorf Computer (32,000 people) and the computer division of Siemens (26,000 people), merged to form Europe's biggest computer company called Siemens Nixdorf information systems (SNI).

The cultures of these businesses were completely different. At Nixdorf we were used to very open communication and regular feedback. The rule was that obvious drawbacks could be openly criticised. At Siemens the feedback culture was very different. They were not used to open critique and questioning things. Asking 'difficult questions' was considered indiscreet behaviour.

I was a member of a working group drafting a new personnel policy for SNI. The former Nixdorf employees, of which I was one, learnt very quickly from a handful of meetings what the new culture was. This new culture, of course, determined in part the new feedback culture of the enterprise and the sort of systems that would work. I returned to Finland in 1991 after a three year assignment only to discover that organisational culture there had also undergone a big change. In fact, such was the scale of that change that the new managing director fired me before we had even got through our first meeting. The company in Finland had also reverted to an old 'command and control' style culture and I could no longer fit myself into that sort of inflexible mindset.

Sometimes development discussions just don't work in a company because the organisational culture is not open enough and there is no established pattern of giving feedback. So, before any new feedback tools are introduced, it is important to consider carefully how these new tools fit into the organisation's culture. But in some situations, the best approach is to try to change the organisation's culture.

The ten commandments of giving feedback

Giving and taking feedback and criticism is a very personal matter. In an effective feedback culture everyone individually needs to appreciate the importance of feedback for their own development and for the wider corporate community. That is why I have listed below the 'ten commandments' of giving feedback that were born out of a feedback training session at Nokia. If we keep these ten commandments in mind, we can promote a positive feedback culture in our own organisation.

1 Give regular feedback
2 Ask feedback for yourself at least as often as you give it.
3 Give feedback immediately when it is called for.
4 Pay attention to and respect the opinions and feedback of others.
5 Give corrective feedback privately, focus on the subject at hand and its effects, and do not put the blame on the individual.
6 Give positive feedback for even the slightest progress and achievement.
7 Agree with the team members what kind of feedback should be given, when and how.
8 Be active, consistent and sincere when giving feedback. This applies to open communication in general.
9 Use feedback to encourage and stimulate the joy of working and the drive to succeed within your own team. Be an example to others.
10 Remember that well-placed and regular feedback is the best and most important leadership tool.

P.S. Remember to give yourself both positive and, if necessary, corrective feedback.

Learning and change

> 'Most transformation programs satisfy themselves with shifting the same old furniture about in the same old room. Some seek to throw some of the furniture away. But real transformation requires that we redesign the room itself. Perhaps even blow up the old room. It requires that we change the thinking behind our thinking – literally, that we learn to rewire our corporate brains.'
>
> Danah Zohar: *ReWiring the Corporate Brain*

Change is learning, development and growth. The following pattern should be implemented in an organisation:

Learning $\geq$ *Change*

Learning should exceed change at all levels. If we manage that we can cope with and even control change.

The difficulty of change

By and large, it isn't easy managing change. On an individual level we can distinguish two different kinds of change: deliberate change and incidental change. Incidental change happens in spite of us and we can only adapt ourselves to it. Deliberate change is voluntary, we have decided to change something ourselves. We have made the choice and the change requires a plan and determined action. Sometimes it is good to stop and think how we have changed ourselves during the last two years. Often we'll discover that we are slaves to a particular way of thinking and have been trying to avoid any change that would complicate our routines. We also notice that even introducing a desired change is often difficult and demands a surprising amount of energy. Just think, for example, about learning something new, taking up a new hobby, quitting smoking or drinking coffee, changing one's eating habits, etc.

If the implementation of change is often difficult and demanding on an individual level, it is probably still harder on a team level. Figure 1.13 shows the degree of difficulty of different forms of change. The acquisition of knowledge is the easiest and takes the least time. Adopting new skills is a little more difficult, while changing attitudes is harder still. The individual's behaviour only changes when all necessary knowledge, skills and attitudes have changed. It is worth remembering that behaviour won't change just because of some acquired knowledge, and that feelings are also important. In his book *Emotional Intelligence* (1997) Daniel Goleman has convincingly demonstrated the importance of feelings in all activities. High level emotional intelligence is very often a factor that can be used to explain some people's success. And just as a change in the collective behaviour requires changed individual behaviour, so a change in the operations of a company requires changed behaviour on all preceding levels.

When we look at Fig. 1.13 we can see that organisational changes are not always easy and contain issues at every different level. That's why change management has become so important. Change management helps in preparing for managing and controlling change.

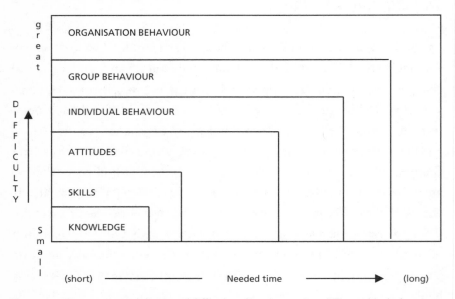

Fig. 1.13   Time range and degree of difficulty of implementing different kind of changes

Slow changes

Another problem is caused by slow changes that we hardly notice. It is called the frog syndrome. When a frog is placed in a kettle filled with lukewarm water, it is perfectly happy. When we put the kettle on a hotplate that slowly warms up the water, the frog is still happy, because the change is so slow that it does not notice it. Only when the water is almost boiling does the poor frog awaken to what is happening and want out. But it is too late by now. Slow changes like this can be a real danger to the organisation and demonstrate why companies need to develop ways of reading weak signals. And, to an extent, the same concerns the whole of society.

The potential for change depends first and foremost on us as individuals. We need to develop our sensitivity, identify our needs and increase our capacity to react to them. We also need to master change as a process. We should understand its different phases and not be afraid of the associated uncertainty. When facing problems we should remember the words of Albert Einstein: 'No problem can be solved on the same level of consciousness as it was born, we must learn to see the world in a different way.' One way of achieving fast and even radical changes is to **raise** the level of consciousness on an individual, a team and an organisational level. This means radically changing the prevailing collective thought processes. We must change the thinking behind our thinking.

Where are we going?

Change is easier if we have a clear vision of where we are going. So do we have a clear vision of the ideal organisation of the future? Well, in my opinion it should be efficient, good at learning and focused on the broad well-being of the stakeholders. In a way **efficiency** is self-evident: no organisation will survive long if it does not work efficiently. It is, however, important that efficiency is understood in the long term. We must be efficient today, next month, next year, after five years, many of us even after twenty years. Real efficiency means that we take care of our own condition and wellbeing. And that's where learning comes in.

A learning organisation means that we can maintain our competencies. We are able to take care of our present duties and develop our competence continuously, always with an eye on future challenges. When we develop our competence today, we are also laying the groundwork for future success. **A 'well-being'** organisation means that people are comfortable in their work. They have a good working motivation – one of the cornerstones of coping with everyday work. Today an efficient organisation is highly dependent on the competence and motivation of its personnel. No enterprise can succeed in the long run if these pieces are not in place.

How to support learning by doing

We have examined learning from various perspectives. Learning is changing, renewal, development, growth and maturing. Learning is a process in which an individual acquires knowledge, skills, attitudes, experiences and contacts that produce changes in his behaviour. Remember the staircase of learning. Learning is knowing, understanding, applying and developing. We can distinguish reactive learning, predictive learning, action learning and transformative learning. An effective learning process includes four phases – experience, evaluation, understanding and application. Different individuals learn in different ways. You can be a pragmatist, reflector, theorist or activist. And there are plenty of obstacles to learning. Remember the concepts of small windows, thick skin, closed gate or wide river.

Learning takes place on an individual, a team and an organisational level. We went through the ten most important learning skills of the organisation – system thinking, mental models, strategic learning, use of feedback systems, self-management, team learning, dialogue, shared vision, exploitation of information systems and sharing knowledge. We underlined the importance of giving feedback behind all development and growth and the difficulty of change.

There is a lot to say about learning, but so what? How do we exploit all this information to the benefit of the company? How do we translate the information into understanding and put it into practice?

We need to establish the sort of models that reinforce the learning process by actually employing that learning. And that means learning while we work. For many people work means continuous studying. As much as 60 percent of working time is learning, according to one survey. This sort of learning on the job, however, has not been modelled in such a way that it could systematically be made more effective. We need to have a closer look at this. I will describe a basic model of learning below.

The basic model for learning by doing

Figure 1.14 shows the basic model of learning by doing. The model offers a simple process to turn our daily working routine into a learning experience. It is based on our basic model of the learning process but has been concretised a

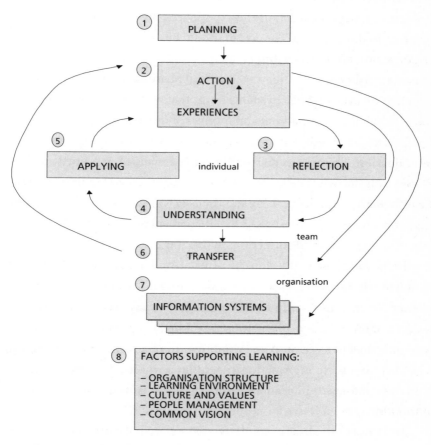

Fig. 1.14 Basic model of learning by doing

little. With the help of systematic planning, action, evaluation, understanding, application and transfer of what we have learnt we can significantly reinforce learning by doing.

Firstly, the basic idea has to be that work is learning and learning is work. Learning and training are investments. We need to ditch any suggestion that training costs and competence is only developed when there is time and money for it. Instead, we should see our everyday duties as opportunities to learn new things and continuously improve our performance.

The first phase is planning. That means anticipating. We need to know what has to be done, the objectives and the skills required. We must continuously look for feedback. We must also be thinking constantly how we can develop our competence and learn new things.

The second phase is action and experiences. 'Well planned is half done' holds true in this case, too. The action should be target-oriented and things need to be put into practice immediately.

The third phase is evaluation, a critical phase of the learning process. Very often we pretend to be in such a hurry that we have no time to plan or properly evaluate the outcomes and motives of our actions.

The fourth phase is understanding what we have determined from our evaluation. This means that actions can be planned, modified and developed with the help of all this newly acquired and digested information. The fifth phase is application. We test the new working method to find out whether it is working or not, basing that judgement on feedback. We can still make minor changes and corrections at this stage.

The sixth phase is the transfer of what we have learnt. We carefully document what we have learnt so we won't forget it and forgo the chance to benefit later. Transfer also means sharing what has been learnt with the members of the team and, ultimately, embedding it in the broader organisational information systems so everybody has immediate access. The seventh phase describes these information systems as a whole – their effectiveness at handling information is an important part of the organisation's overall competence.

And the eighth phase reminds us what we need in place to support the learning process. It is important that the structure of the organisation sup-

ports learning and that the organisation has a favourable learning environment. The culture and values of the organisation as well as human resource
management need to underpin these structures. Common vision supports
common learning.

The main processes supporting organisational learning

Organisational learning should be promoted wherever possible. It can be
supported with the help of performance management, competence management and knowledge management. And these should be regarded as
basic processes of an intelligent organisation that can either be separate or
built inside each other.

Performance management is one of the most important processes in
a well-run organisation. It combines agreement on objectives, coaching,
result evaluation and development into elements connected to each other
in a continuous process aiming at improving the performance of the organisation by developing individuals and teams. Performance management
means simply that everyone knows what their function is, what are their
personal objectives, what kind of competence is required of them and that
they get enough coaching and feedback in order to be able to take care of
their duties. The tasks of the organisation are the starting point of performance management. A well working performance management system creates the basis for other processes.

Competence management is becoming increasingly important, because competence plays such an important role in today's competitive environment. It means aligning the core competence of the firm with its essential vision and strategy. That's what will define competitive advantage. It
needs closely monitoring against a target level, which thereafter enables us
to make the necessary development plans that must be implemented and
converted to personal development plans of the individuals. The starting
point of competence management is the vision and strategy of the organisation: this is maybe the only factor separating competence management from
traditional development and training activity.

The objective of knowledge management is the continuous and effective application of new information. As the amount and importance of information is increasing, so knowledge management becomes one of the factors in success. It means that we can systematically create, receive, store, distribute and apply information. Information technology is key here but it is always worth remembering that the critical part of the job is people-facing. The cornerstone of knowledge management is in a way the competence and experience of the organisation made available to the whole organisation.

These processes are examined in detail in the separate chapters of this book. I particularly want to show how they relate to one another and to discuss how they might be combined to produce one totally restructured process.

Chapter 2
Performance Management

'Performance management, like Kennedy's speech, is an act of communication that empowers people to rise up to a calling that's bigger than themselves – not the tool of Orwellian dictators. As an ongoing process of planning, coaching, reviewing and rewarding, it can inspire people to reach for goals as momentous as putting a man on the moon.'

David C. McClelland

Continuous improvement of performance as an objective

Performance management is the most important of the human resource management processes, not least because it lays the foundations for most of the other human resource functions. It has been used by organisations for a long time but it does not, in practice, generally work very well. In essence, it means the individual, the team and the whole organisation know:

- what is the purpose of their operations;
- what are the key objectives;
- how the feedback systems work; and
- what kind of competence is needed.

Its aim is the continuous improvement of performance (see Fig. 2.1) and involves combining the efforts and objectives of the organisation and the individual. It needs assessing from the viewpoint of the organisation, individual and environment.

There are four elements in the performance management process:

- setting objectives;
- follow-up/coaching;
- feedback; and
- development.

Originally the term performance appraisal was used to describe performance management. It was mainly about setting objectives and giving feedback based on those benchmarks. The emphasis was on evaluation. And that, unfortunately, was why it was perceived by a lot of people as an essentially negative exercise. No one likes being judged like that.

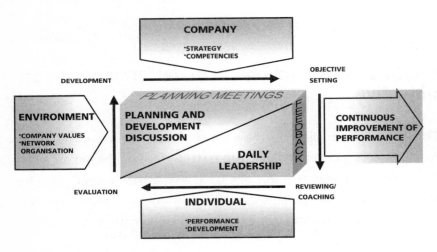

Fig. 2.1 The framework for performance management

The term performance management, a later accretion, implies something a bit more – it suggests some follow-up coaching and development. The focus is transferred from past to present and future, and from evaluation to development. It has been an important change, still not fully understood by a lot of organisations.

Performance management takes place on the level of the individual, the team and the whole organisation. The most important tools are planning meetings, planning and development discussions, and daily leadership. Planning meetings are needed when operations are led at the level of team, department or organisation, while planning and development discussions are generally conducted on an individual level. And sitting on top of these is daily leadership, laying the foundation for effective performance management. If daily leadership is badly managed, planning and development discussions are almost bound to fail.

The objective of performance management is continuous improvement. This can be an improvement in customer satisfaction, operational efficiency, or just the way employees feel about their work. It is a long-term, and continuous process.

Performance management needs to be planned over a specific timeframe, ideally about six months. We call that periodic planning to distinguish it from the more familiar planning functions like budgeting or long-term planning.

Because it is such an important process, its ownership is best shared. It is not just HR property. In fact, the main owners are the line managers. And individuals have an important part to play in the process, too. Planning and development discussions are only effective if all the participants share some responsibility for the output. An effective working performance management process and, particularly, planning and development discussions are a starting point for many other human resource management processes, like training and development, career and succession planning, and rewarding. Figure 2.2 shows performance management in a nutshell. It presents the most important units of the process:

- objectives;
- target group;
- sub-processes;
- time period;
- tools;
- owners; and
- starting points and connections.

Every organisation should go through these dimensions and define their own solutions. It will help in building a successful performance management system.

OBJECTIVES	CONTINUOUS IMPROVEMENT OF PERFORMANCE			
	CUSTOMER SATISFACTION	OPERATIVE EFFICIENCY	COMPETENCE	WELLBEING
TARGET GROUP	Individual	Team	Department	Organisation
SUB-PROCESSES	Objective setting	Reviewing/coaching	Feedback	Development
TIME PERIOD	Period planning:	Twice a year		
TOOLS	Daily leadership	Planning and development discussions	Planning meetings	Team's planning discussions
OWNER	Individual	Manager	Department manager	Top management
STARTING POINT/ CONNECTIONS	Training and development process	Rewarding-process	Career and succession planning	etc.

Fig. 2.2 Performance management in a nutshell

Different viewpoints

The viewpoint of the organisation

The idea of performance management is to combine the viewpoints of the organisation, the individual and the environment. Its objectives should be consistent throughout the whole organisation. It can be used to harmonise objectives where they have been allowed to fall into conflict. Figure 2.3 illustrates this.

Situation A   Situation B

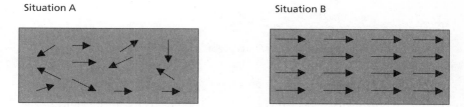

Fig. 2.3   The goal is to harmonise the objectives

This is, in fact, one of the key tasks of performance management. It often works best to this end where it is clearly connected to other planning processes of the organisation. Figure 2.4 shows these connections, starting from strategic planning. With the help of performance management, it is possible to work from strategic management through to operational management; from a vision to the practical dimension and the development of the operational process. It should be noted that the two-way arrows in Fig. 2.4 work in both directions. Performance management can be seen as a management process from top down, but it is just as important to see it as a feedback process working from bottom to top.

It is, of course, important that the purpose of the operations, key task areas, key objectives and critical competence are clear on all organisational levels. To that end, performance management is a key part of the management system of the organisation.

The viewpoint of the individual

The individual needs to understand how he or she fits into the organisation's

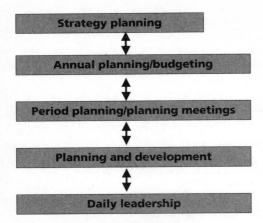

Fig. 2.4 Connecting performance management to strategic management

larger entity: how does what I do relate to what the company does? We should all be able to answer this question. It helps us to do the right things and achieve top results. Arranging bricks, building a brick wall or build the world's biggest cathedral. Top performance means climbing some steps to get to the top.

First of all, we should know the vision of the whole organisation and the objectives of our own unit. This helps us to see the purpose of our own duties. We should also weigh the purpose of our tasks against the values and culture of the organisation. These give us an insight into how we usually operate. Then we need to know what are our key tasks and what skills we need to complete them. Without sufficient competence we cannot perform our tasks well. And lastly we must have clear objectives and be committed to these objectives. That's the only effective way we can reach the top performance level in our own organisation. An effective performance management process should provide the individual with this kind of a model to analyse his own top performance. Figure 2.5 shows the steps to reaching the most productive operation.

A performance management process should also offer the individual possibilities to develop his/her own performance and competence. The development of the individual should be assessed both in the short term and in the long term. Short-term development means mainly task-based development. Long-term development means the advancement of the individual in his/her career and discussing different career plans.

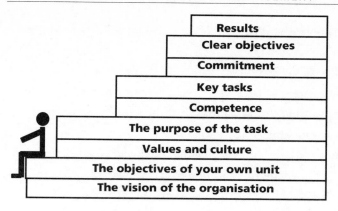

Fig. 2.5 How can an individual achieve good results?

Viewpoint of the environment

Environmental factors include the values and culture of the organisation and the organisational structure. The culture of the organisation affects the practical implementation of the discussions about planning and development. If there is a good feedback culture within the organisation and people are used to regular and open feedback, then it is likely to affect the outcome of these discussions. In contrast, if the culture is very hierarchical and the management style overbearing then it can be useless trying to establish a two-way feedback system. And if planning and development discussions do not work well in an organisation, it is worth looking at the culture of the organisation and working out how it supports or prevents this kind of thing.

Because the values and culture of the organisation are so important to how it works they need to be an integral part of the conduct of planning and development discussion. Values should be examined and made concrete; what do they actually mean on a practical level, how do we follow them, how should our operations be altered to conform to them better? Evaluating them should always be a part of the discussion and questions like these should be asked:

- What are the basic values of our organisation?
- How do they appear in practice?
- How do I implement these values in practice?
- How should I alter my way of working to conform better to the values?

- How does my superior and my whole department follow the values of our organisation?

Only when the values are discussed and we try to define them together can they start to steer our operations. Failing that, they will remain simply an abstract management ideology and jargon.

Figure 2.6 shows an example of how the intelligent organisation conducts its value discussions. This organisation has six values. The implementation of these values is evaluated from the perspective of the employee, superior and the whole department. The discussion will focus on the definition of three measures with which the values can better be implemented in the future.

How do you see these 12 aspects of the values of the organisation (Fig. 2.6) reflected in a) your own behaviour b) your manager's behaviour c) generally in your department? Both the employee and the manager should give their evaluation beforehand and then analyse it together in their discussion. After that it is very important to define some action points on how to improve the situation. The purpose of including the values in PD discussion is to make them more concrete in the everyday working environment and constantly develop the organisation. (The scale: 1= unsatisfactory, 5= outstanding.)

no	Criterion	Employee	Manager	Department
	CUSTOMER SATISFACTION			
1	Discovering customer needs	1 2 3 4 5	1 2 3 4 5	1 2 3 4 5
2	Respecting and caring for the customers	1 2 3 4 5	1 2 3 4 5	1 2 3 4 5
	RESPECT FOR THE INDIVIDUAL			
3	Fair treatment on all occasions	1 2 3 4 5	1 2 3 4 5	1 2 3 4 5
4	Acceptance of diversity	1 2 3 4 5	1 2 3 4 5	1 2 3 4 5
	TEAM WORK			
5	Appreciation of team work	1 2 3 4 5	1 2 3 4 5	1 2 3 4 5
6	Supporting other team members	1 2 3 4 5	1 2 3 4 5	1 2 3 4 5
	ACHIEVEMENT			
7	Shared vision and goals	1 2 3 4 5	1 2 3 4 5	1 2 3 4 5
8	Feedback and appreciation	1 2 3 4 5	1 2 3 4 5	1 2 3 4 5
	KNOWLEDGE SHARING			
9	Active sharing of knowledge	1 2 3 4 5	1 2 3 4 5	1 2 3 4 5
10	Independent searching of new knowledge	1 2 3 4 5	1 2 3 4 5	1 2 3 4 5
	CONTINUOUS LEARNING			
11	Innovativeness and courage	1 2 3 4 5	1 2 3 4 5	1 2 3 4 5
12	Humble and open mind	1 2 3 4 5	1 2 3 4 5	1 2 3 4 5

Fig. 2.6 Values as a part of planning and development discussions
What are the three most important action points based on the above analysis?

1 _____

2 _____

3 _____

The way an organisation supports its performance management is also important. The hierarchical organisations that have been typical in the past make efficient top down communication possible but they don't work so well in other respects. Today we are more likely to be working in a network and process organisation. The explicit superior-subordinate relations are maybe not so self-explanatory in these instances. We might, for example, have more than one superior. So with whom do we have our planning and development discussions? We should pay attention to the form taken by the organisation and the way it operates when planning a performance management system and tailoring it to the needs of the organisation.

Planning and development discussions

'It is not worth being disappointed with people, if they don't do as you have thought. If you get cynical you need a break. Otherwise you don't have the energy to go on. You must admit this, it is part of the business. Not even a play can be produced without crises.'

Asko Sarkola, director, Helsinki City Theatre

Objectives

Planning and development discussions are the single most important tool of performance management. They are called by various names: superior-subordinate -discussion, development discussion, discussion on objectives, result discussion etc. The term planning and development discussion is used in this book because it describes best the nature of these discussions. The objective is the evaluation, planning and development of the performance of the individual.

The planning and development discussion (PD) should be a systematic event repeated (normally twice a year) between the employee and the manager in order to improve performance and open communication.

There are five concrete objectives in the PD discussion:

1   Evaluate the results achieved.
2   Set objectives for the next working period.

3   Define development needs and make an individual development plan.
4   Develop the co-operation between the superior and the subordinate.
5   Enhance general working conditions and climate.

It is of utmost importance that both parties understand the purpose and objectives of these discussions. If one doesn't understand what they are about, why they are important and what their role is, it is very unlikely that they will serve any purpose. It is worth dedicating enough time to determining and communicating the purpose. Understanding what they are for is even more important than the detail of the discussion.

The contents

The performance management process should include, among other things, a confidential planning and development discussion held twice a year between the employee and his or her superior. The aim of these discussions is to improve performance, develop the individual and further the practice of open and direct communication. During the planning and development discussion it is also important to update the person's job description and training records. Separate forms have been produced as an aid to discussions (model forms are attached as appendices). But even when forms are used as aids during discussions, the manager should aim to hold the discussion in an informal, open and flexible atmosphere. The contents of the planning and development discussion are shown in Fig. 2.7.

The objectives of the planning discussion should include the following:

- to ensure that the individual's actions are consistent with the objectives of the company as a whole;
- to reach mutual understanding regarding job content, main focus areas, objectives and the basis for the evaluation of results;
- to reach a common view on how well the individual's results from the preceding working period match the agreed objectives; and
- to learn from experience and find a better base for future planning and development.

I Evaluation review

1 Meeting personal objectives

2 General performance (team work, knowledge sharing, positive attitude etc.)

3 Factors which have contributed to/obstructed the achievement of objectives

4 Values and modes of operation

II Objective setting

1 Job description/purpose of the job

2 Key task areas

3 Key objectives

4 Key competencies for the job

III Development review

1 Employee's own objectives and opinions

2 Manager's expectations

3 Personal development plan

4 Long-term development plan

5 Total health/well-being

IV Key learning points

1 What did we learn from the discussion?

2 How can we improve it in the future?

Fig. 2.7 The contents of the planning and development discussions

We are looking at development both in the current job and in the career in general. The discussion should identify the skills required in the current job and determines the development needs of the individual in these areas. A personal, written development plan can be drawn up and, if necessary, a copy sent to the training manager. The discussion about career development is not career planning per se, but more an opportunity to crystallise the individual's expectations and motivation. 'What do I want and why?'

These expectations are weighed against the opportunities the company can offer.

Preparing oneself for the discussions

For a successful development discussion both the manager and the employee must prepare themselves thoroughly and go through the matters to be covered in some detail. The manager should do the following:

- fix the date at least one week in advance;
- give the employee clear instructions on how to prepare;
- reserve a quiet place and ensure that the discussion is not interrupted; and
- reserve sufficient time for the discussion (about two hours) bearing in mind both the manager's and the employee's experience of these discussions.

Below there is a list of things that should be covered in a planning and development discussion and prepared beforehand.

1   Assessment of the preceding working period and feedback to the employee on his/her performance
    - How well did the employee achieve the objectives set for him/her?
    - How was the general performance; supporting others, team work, knowledge sharing etc.?
    - How well were the values of the organisation followed by the person, the team and the whole department?
    - What factors had a significant impact on the achievement or non-achievement of the objectives?
    - How did the manager's own behaviour bear on the achievements of the employee?
2   Reviewing the job description
    - What is the purpose of the job today?

- What are the employee's key responsibilities?
- How should the job description be altered to bring it in line with current practice?

3 Agreeing on objectives for the next planning period
- What are the main objectives for the coming period?
- What is the timetable?
- What is the required support, follow-up and reporting?

4 Evaluation of the manager's role and cooperation within the team
- How successful was the manager in his/her manager role and how could he/she develop it?
- What is the prevailing atmosphere among team members?
- Are there some other actual and relevant issues?

5 Making the development plan
- What are the key competencies for this job?
- What are the development needs?
- How can we prioritise those?
- How are development actions planned?

6 Discussing long-term career plans
- What are the individual's long-term expectations about his/her work?
- How much is the person willing to invest in his/her development?
- What are the organisation's needs concerning the employee's development?

7 Discussion about the overall well-being of the work community
- How is the person and the working community performing and developing?
- What is the situation concerning overall well-being: professional, physical, mental, social and spiritual condition?

8 Key learning points
- What did we learn from the PD discussion process?
- PD discussion should be seen as a powerful learning instrument, where we give and get feedback in order to improve our performance.

Rules of the game

At its best, the planning and development discussion is a confidential talk between two mature people of equal standing. The following ten principles should be adhered to in these discussions:

1 Use a quiet negotiation room.
2 Decisions should be agreed upon, not imposed.
3 Express your views honestly and directly.
4 Begin the review of the past period with positive feedback. Negative or critical feedback is then easier to handle later.
5 Be an active listener. A basic skill behind successful dialogue is listening.
6 Every decision should include an action plan, timetable and person responsible.
7 In the discussion you should not criticise other people.
8 Prepare thoroughly for the discussion.
9 Do not allow the discussion to become a negotiation over salary; the aim is to review work performance and to find ways to improve it further. If it is felt that the salary or other benefits should be discussed, this could be done in a separate discussion.
10 Try to find constructive solutions to disagreements.

Different phases of discussion

A planning and development discussion can be outlined in six phases – a six-part drama played twice a year. I have used a variety of ways to train supervisors how to manage these discussions and have had the best success with a training programme where we – I and our training manager – demonstrated phase by phase the discussion we had ourselves. We both explained our own visions and experiences and presented the final results of the discussion. This kind of planning and development discussion play made things more concrete and gave a good example of how to implement it in practice. It is important to understand the purpose of the discussion, your own role in it, and the exact handling order of things. Figure 2.8 shows briefly the different phases of the discussion.

Successful discussion requires thorough preparation. Both parties must prepare well. This way we can concentrate on the essentials in the discussion and save time.

The opening phase of the discussion means creating a pleasant atmosphere for the discussion. The discussion should be started with a subject of common interest. It is also good to make sure that the purpose of the discussion is understood and preparations made carefully.

After this follows the evaluation or assessment phase. It is often a good idea to start with the subordinate presenting his/her own evaluation of the situation, how well their targets have been met and how they have been achieved. Very often the superior has only a summarising role in this situation. In this phase the subordinate should speak more and let the superior comment and complete the subordinate's own evaluation. It is important to

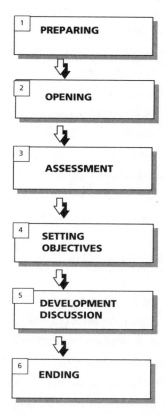

Fig. 2.8   Different phases of planning and development discussions

consider together what we can learn on the basis of this joint evaluation. In the evaluation attention should also be paid to future activities.

A discussion on the purpose of the job should be conducted in the phase when the objectives are defined. What kind of value added does my job give to the whole organisation? In this phase it is also good to define the key duties. There is no reason to list everything. It's more effective to concentrate on the essentials and perhaps consider how much time we spend with each area. Then define the key objectives, maybe the ten most important for the upcoming period. When key duties and objectives have been defined it is worth considering what kind of competence is needed for perfect performance. This is when the competence profile is drafted. The profile should be drawn from the viewpoint of the organisation and the job itself before the definition of a personal development plan.

In the development discussion phase a concrete personal development plan is put togetherfor the subordinate. It is also worth considering here the subordinate's and superior's expectations for the future as well as the long-term plans of the subordinate.

It is advisable to end with a summary to make sure that both parties share a similar view of what has been discussed. It should also be confirmed that the discussion has been documented properly and that the forward-looking measures were clearly agreed upon. Only this way can we achieve joint commitment to agreed actions. And it is always important that the discussion be ended in a positive tone, even if there have been some disagreements in the different phases of the discussion.

Possible problems

Planning and development discussions do not always succeed. A discussion that fails can be very frustrating to both parties and diminish work motivation for a long time. That is why enough attention should be paid to the quality of the discussions. Some kind of 'control system' should be established in each organisation to safeguard the implementation of the discussions and their good quality and to guarantee that everybody has the necessary competence to participate in the discussions.

One way to handle this quality control is to collect reports from superiors after each planning and development discussion round. The superiors have to answer the following type of questions:

1   How many subordinates do you have?
2   How many of them have you had a development discussion with?
3   When did you have this discussion?
4   How much time did you use for this discussion?
5   If you had no such discussion with any/some of your subordinates, why was this?
6   What is your total evaluation concerning the success of the discussions (scale of grades 1–10)?
7   What issues did you find problematic in the planning and development discussions?
8   What are the fields you need training in?
9   With how many subordinates did you agree upon a development target aiming at improving the critical skills of your whole department?

A summary of a report like this is fairly good at determining how the planning and development discussions work in an organisation. And from that it should be easy to implement the necessary development measures.

Figure 2.9 lists the most common problems in the planning and development discussions. The biggest is that the purpose of the discussion is not understood and the attitude towards the discussion is negative. Poor preparation is also a general problem. Giving and receiving feedback is also surprisingly difficult. This is often connected to insufficient interaction skills. We are unable to create the openness required in these discussions and unable to handle conflicts. The definition of the targets is also often clearly problematic.

Planning and development discussions are not always easy. At their best these discussions contain creative dialogue, at worst the parties are blaming each other and speaking over the top of each other. In order to succeed well these discussions require good interaction skills from both sides.

1 Poor preparation by the subordinate/superior.

2 Rapid staff turnover/the superior changes too often.

3 Development plan is a 'list of hopes' and is not necessarily connected to competencies required in the job.

4 Involvement of the subordinate (does not speak) + feedback.

5 Routine procedure, too similar targets.

6 Matrix organisation: subordinates work for other projects.

7 Difficult to concretise the link to competencies and competence classification.

8 Discussion on values difficult.

9 Subordinates not aware of job circulation possibilities/processes.

10 Hostile attitude of the subordinate.

11 Evaluation of the competency level of the subordinate is difficult.

12 Connection to salary unclear.

13 Tolerance of critique insufficient.

14 Discussion with people from different cultures is difficult.

Fig. 2.9 Problems that emerge in planning and development discussions

The parties must also have the ability to confront conflicts. One should not be afraid of disagreement but aim to face and resolve it.

I will give you two examples from my own experience. During the past 20 years I have myself conducted approximately 40 discussions like this in the role of a subordinate and a few hundred as a superior and I think I have mastered their purpose. However, there will always be surprises and difficult situations; conflicts and negative feelings.

Once I was having this kind of discussion with a new subordinate. She had been in the job for four years. She had many good qualities, but there were also areas that clearly needed to be developed. Her skill to carry things through was weak, she was easily stressed and cooperation with others was difficult at times. I had decided that I would openly take up these development targets in the discussion with her. When I started to go through them she reacted badly. She burst into tears and started to blame me. She was not used to being treated like this. I tried to calm her down, but the discussion did not proceed smoothly. I explained that we clearly had conflicting views and that we should think about this a little. I suggested we continue the discussion the following afternoon. When we met again the situation had calmed down and we could move on. This time she was better able to take some of the feedback. A few weeks later she came to my room and said she wanted to talk further about this incident. She told me that for the first time in her career she had received honest, critical feedback and, with hindsight, she was very grateful. It had felt awful at first, but after a few weeks of mulling it over she realised it had been accurate and that it would be useful to her future development. Maybe this incident partly contributed to the very positive development of our future cooperation.

Another example is drawn from my working experience in Germany. I had been there for about a year when my own superior, who had brought me there to work for him, suddenly left the company. I got a new 'true German' superior whom I didn't know very well. After we had worked together for about six months, I felt it was not going to work out. We had major differences of opinion about how best to develop the international personnel operations, and our working styles were entirely different. We also had contrasting personalities. When we had the development discussion, I told him that in my opinion we weren't cooperating very effectively and I said that I wanted a new boss. This kind of open and direct criticism was a bit too much for him. The German working culture is somewhat more formal and hierarchic than the one we are used to in Finland. He told me it would be better if I packed my bags and left the country. That is how the conversation ended. We continued our discussion the next day on a more formal but still very cool basis. But over the next few weeks we expanded the discussions to include his superior and eventually found a kind of compromise. We managed, after a while, to find some sort of mutual agreement. And from there onwards, our cooperation was very fruitful. These two examples should illustrate the value of confronting differences of opinion. There is no need to be afraid of disagreement as long as you are prepared to work towards a creative and positive solution.

Consider Jouko Lönngvist's brilliant analysis of the way people really respond to management by objectives. 'As an ideology, management by objectives is based on a concept that expects people to be sensible and formal, conscious of their endeavours and provided with good morals. This thinking pattern is based on a slightly naïve concept of people who plan, make agreements and implement them in a way agreed upon. The problem will be that people, in addition, often think rather irrationally and have conflicting views, feel strongly and often also express these feelings, are not aware of their endeavours and the motives of these endeavours and have also very different moral conceptions. Because of these factors, the straightforward target thinking is not implemented in practical working life as easily as one could expect.' It is good to keep this viewpoint in mind and remember that everyone of us is different.

Factors behind success

It is important to be aware of the problems associated with development discussions and overcome them with the help of sufficient training, instruction and consultation. It is also important to know what makes these discussions a success. The following is a summary of these most important success factors.

1 The superior is himself/herself well prepared for the discussion and gives his/her subordinates enough instructions in advance to prepare for the discussion.
2 The subordinate is well prepared, understands his/her own active role and handles his or her side of the discussion well.
3 In the discussion situation the superior listens actively, the atmosphere is open and it is easy for the subordinate to express his/her own views.
4 During the discussion, issues are handled on a practical level and the parties confirm, if necessary, that things have been understood in the same way.
5 During the discussion both parties learn something new that improves their performance in the future.

6 The development of the cooperation between the subordinate and the superior and in the whole team is openly handled during the discussion.

7 The superior is willing to receive feedback and asks for it actively.

8 The discussions have been connected correctly with other management processes.

9 A concrete personal development plan is drafted for the subordinate during the discussion.

10 The necessary decisions are made as a result of the discussions and action plans to which both parties commit themselves are clearly agreed upon.

Figure 2.10 shows a list of the basic factors for the planning and development discussions. This list also acts as a good checklist when evaluating their success. The present state, strengths, weaknesses and development needs of the discussions can be listed by company and unit and give individual superiors concrete feedback on the discussions held.

---

1 *Discussion atmosphere*. Discussion atmosphere was open and also problems could be taken up with the superior.

2 *Going through the total situation*. The superior explained the total situation and objectives of both the company and our own unit/department.

3 *Feedback and evaluation of performance*. Meeting targets and job performance was evaluated in the discussion. The superior thanked staff for good performance and also gave feedback for bad performance.

4 *Targets and development of work*. The duties, objectives and action plans of the subordinates as well as the development of the work, duties and operation requirements were sufficiently handled in the discussions.

5 *Decision-making and agreeing on different matters*. The discussion resulted in necessary decisions and schedules, action plans and the follow-up

---

of their implementation were agreed upon. The matters agreed upon were recorded for the use of both parties.

6 *Development of the subordinate.* The development of the subordinate was sufficiently handled during the discussions (how he/she had developed himself/herself and reached the learning target) as well as the training and development needs for the future (competency and learning needs).

7 *Fairness of the superior.* The superior evaluated the performance of the subordinate fairly and took the subordinate's views into consideration when making the decisions.

8 *Mode of interaction of the superior.* In the discussion situation the superior listened, but also openly introduced his/her own views and opinions. The discussions concentrated on the essentials. The same issues are also discussed in between the actual planning and development discussions.

9 *Building of cooperation.* During the discussion the working cooperation between the superior and the subordinate was handled thoroughly and on a sufficiently concrete level. The superior himself/herself was willing to receive feedback and also to discuss the strengths, weaknesses and development needs of his/her own management style.

10 *Creating the conditions for the discussion.* Enough time was reserved for the discussion. All disturbance was eliminated. The superior gave sufficient instructions in advance for the preparation and was also well preparaed for the discussion himself/herself.

11 *Contribution of the subordinates* (the subordinates' own evaluations). The subordinates had prepared for the discussion and handled well their own part of the discussion.

(Copyright Psycho-Sociologic Research Institute, PSYKO GROUP 1994)

Fig. 2.10 Basic factors of the planning and development discussions (question groups of PSYKO's evaluation on how well the planning and development discussions are working)

It is important to offer enough training for these planning and development discusssions. We should also make sure that the purpose of the discussions has been understood and that all the members of the organisation have the necessary competence required to get the best out of them. It is not enough that superiors are well grounded in the techniques. Subordinates also need to be trained.

Plenty of training, both internal and external, has traditionally been made available for the superiors. But a successful discussion cannot be conducted alone, if the other partner is reluctant. That is why subordinates also benefit from training.

It is often effective and convenient to train superiors and subordinates at the same time. It can produce an enlightening insight into the different focus of the various roles. Set up the training at an appropriate moment, for example just before the discussions. Good results have been achieved when the training has been given in mixed groups just before the beginning of the discussion round. The training consists mainly of repeating the basic things and analysing some of the more problematic areas. It need only last two or three hours and it is easy for all parties concerned to participate. Of course, superiors would also benefit from longer sessions.

Planning and development discussions for teams

Because we act and work more and more in teams, we can ask whether planning and development discussions should also be conducted in teams. Discussions held on a team level can be useful for example when:

- the team has joint objectives and tasks;
- individual objectives are hard to set; and
- the work is mainly done in a team.

Team discussions can complement individual discussions, but should not replace them. They should concentrate mainly on the definition of objectives, evaluation of joint results, issues concerning the division of the workload, and evaluation of how the team generally works.

Appendix 3 shows an example of a form for the planning and development discussion for a team. The agenda might, for example, include issues like:

- members of the team;
- purpose of the team;
- suppliers and customers of the team;
- key tasks, objectives and indicators of success;
- competencies needed in the team;
- operating conditions of the team;
- controlling the team;
- rules of the game for the team; and
- development plan for the team.

Many of the same issues are handled in well-run planning meetings. Indeed, this kind of discussion can easily form part of a general planning meeting. It should be possible to combine new practices with old tools so that we don't overburden the organisation with too many meetings and discussions.

By making a summary of individual planning and development discussions and by distributing it to all the members of the team, the whole team can distribute valuable information about the duties and objectives of the members of the team. In our own team we have used a form called 'Managing your own job' that has worked very well. Everyone fills in three basic things concerning his/her own job:

- What is the purpose of my job?
- What are my key tasks (time share in percentage)?
- What are my key objectives (ten most important objectives)?

The distribution of this kind of information within the team helps the members of the team to cooperate better and to support each other.

Daily leadership and planning meetings

'Reflection doesn't take anything away from decisiveness, from being a person of action. In fact, it generates the inner toughness that you need to be an effective person of action – to be a leader.'

Peter Koestenbaum

Excellent performance management is built on daily leadership, planning meetings and planning and development discussions. And these are all closely linked to the strategic management and yearly planning of the organisation. Figure 2.11 shows a working practice of performance management.

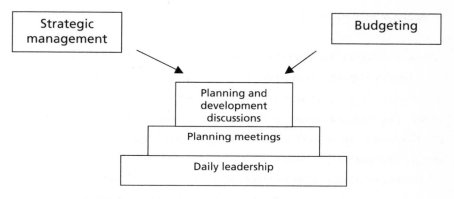

Fig. 2.11   The practice of performance management

Daily leadership forms the basis of both planning meetings and planning and development discussions. At the same time these tools direct, support and steer daily leadership.

Daily leadership

Daily leadership is all about directing and supporting the subordinates, giving feedback, coaching, delegating and doing things together. Good daily leadership means that the superior knows his/her subordinates and knows how to manage them individually and fairly, and knows how to motivate them.

Good performance management is built on good daily leadership. A summary of the effectiveness of daily leadership is made in the planning and development discussions. These two complement and support each other.

Traditionally management is planning, organising, motivating and controlling. It takes place on many different levels. Here are the six levels of management:

- managing yourself;
- leadership (individuals, teams);
- management;
- managing markets;
- technological management; and
- strategic management.

A good manager can steer operations effectively on all these levels.

Leadership or human resource management has become more and more important. The people are the most important resource of an organisation. The competitiveness of the organisation is mainly built on the competence and motivation of its staff. Managing this precious resource is, quite simply, essential.

It has become one of the most important areas of competence for the manager. He or she must achieve results with people and with the help of people. The responsibility for this practical human resource management has increasingly been transferred to line managers. The role of the personnel function is to support the line organisation in this work.

The manager has many areas of responsibility in this critical sphere. They include:

- recruiting;
- introduction;
- performance management;
- training and development;
- rewarding;
- competence management;
- knowledge management;
- communication;
- development of the working community; and
- change management.

In all these areas the key element is about managing people. It requires a skill with people, an ability to communicate, to interact with people and do things with them, solve problems and make decisions, develop the team, act as an example, show purpose and make others follow. Leadership is one of the most difficult areas of management. It is as much art as science. And it takes time to bring up a good leader.

Skilful human resource managment is a precondition of the success of an organisation. In a sense, the manager's duty is to organise success. And the manager has only succeeded, if his/her team has succeeded. Still, most organisations seem to have one common problem: human resource management doesn't work. There is a striking lack of competence in this area.

The need for people skills is equally imperative at every level of the organisation. Of course, we need conceptual competence in the organisation – strategic thinking – identifying requirements and seeing opportunity have traditionally been emphasised in top management. Today these skills are required from practically everyone in high tech-companies. Then there is technical competence, an emphasis on the operational level of every organisation. But competence with people is needed on all levels of the organisation (see Fig. 2.12). That is why we should invest more in developing people skills. It means improving the management of people.

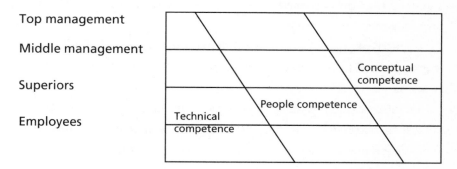

Fig. 2.12 The importance of different competence areas in an organisation

Skilful human resource management can have a great impact on the employees' motivational level. But equally, motivation has a big influence on performance level. According to the pioneering motivational studies of William James, our performance level is 20–30 percent below our ideal performance level when our motivation level is low. But, if our motivational level is high, we can achieve 80–90 percent of our ideal performance level. Good motivation is thus extremely important for top performance. Fig. 2.13 illustrates the effect of the motivation level on the performance of the individual.

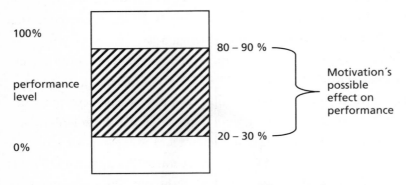

Fig. 2.13 The role of motivation on the level of individual performance

Well-balanced daily leadership helps us to keep the motivation level of the employees as high as possible. For that reason alone, the success of daily leadership and how to develop it should always be discussed in the planning and development meetings.

Different organisations use different leadership models. It is of utmost importance that performance management forms an integral part of these models.

One model that has already been used for a long time and is still used is situational leadership, conceived by Paul Hersey and Kenneth H. Blanchard. It basically provides a set of tools with which to assess the ability of employees and dictates a management style according to the corresponding categories.

Situational leadership is a good example of a model that effectively combines performance management and planning and development discussions. The evaluation of the subordinate's readiness level plays a very important role in the situational leadership model. The model combines four readiness levels with four corresponding management styles. The readiness level of the subordinate can be high and he/she is able and motivated to perform a certain task. If the readiness level is low, the subordinate is unable and unwilling to contribute. The model describes four different leadership styles, i.e. telling, selling, participating and delegating. These styles must be applied according to the readiness level of the subordinate. Fig. 2.14 illustrates the idea.

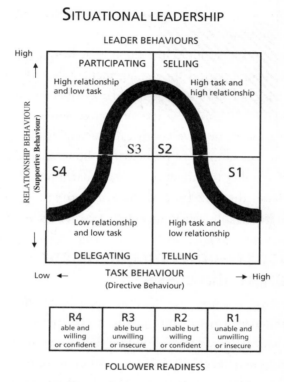

Fig. 2.14   Situational leadership model (Hersey and Blanchard)

It is important that the daily leadership within the organisation is steered by a conscious leadership model. The relationship between this model and performance management and planning and development discussions should also clearly be indicated. Only this way can we continue to develop the way the company manages people.

Planning meetings

Planning meetings are an important part of performance management, particularly on a departmental level. We use them to plan, set objectives, follow the implementation of objectives, define critical competence and make development plans. Planning meetings play an important role in the following chain: budgeting – planning meetings – planning and development discussions – daily leadership.

Planning meetings should be held at least twice a year. They should be seen as an integral part of the management system. They need a clear function directing operations. They should not just be routine meetings but instead should include some new and innovative elements.

It is also essential that everybody can participate in the meetings and influence them. The number of participants should not be too big so that the individual's ability to influence is not undermined. Twenty or thirty people is probably the maximum. If there are more people in the department, these meetings can be held separately for each section or team.

Connections to other human resource management processes

Performance management is the most important process of human resource management and a precondition for the success of the organisation. It is used to make sure that the whole organisation is continuously developing its activities and it is linked to all sorts of other processes, as described in Fig. 2.15.

Performance management must clearly be connected to the strategic planning and budgeting systems of the organisation if it is to work in practice. It should also be closely connected to competence management and knowledge management. And performance management needs to be linked to areas of personnel management like training and development, rewarding and career planning.

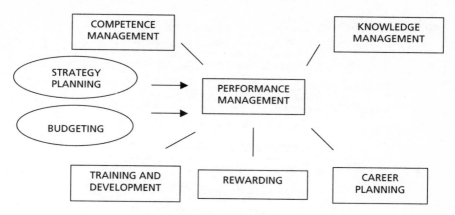

Fig. 2.15 Performance management connections to other processes

Training and development

The links with training and development processes are quite obvious. The organisation must continuously make sure that the right skill sets are available. A personal development plan is drafted for everybody in the planning and development discussions that lists their individual needs. And a summary of these needs determines the budget for the organisation's training program.

Rewarding

The link between performance management and reward is not always straightforward. Firstly, when we talk about rewarding we need to remember that rewarding is much more than just salary, as Fig. 2.16 illustrates. Salary is, of course, important, but it is not the only motivating factor. Moreover, salary is a factor that can easily cause discontent. It is worth bearing in mind the other reward tools shown in Fig. 2.16 when rewarding someone for good performance. Positive feedback, development opportunities and challenging duties are factors that can keep up work satisfaction in the long term.

Fig. 2.16   Different ways of rewarding

A working performance management system requires that:

- the performance clearly affects the salary;
- good performance will be better rewarded than average performance; and
- poor performance is not tolerated in the long run.

We should be able to demonstrate a clear connection between an individual's performance and their reward and make sure it is implemented in practice. Figure 2.17 demonstrates how good performance and other factors affect the reward process. Other essential factors that influence the salary level include task area, competence, experience and seniority. Competence-based salary systems have emerged lately, but while that is an important factor in the determination of salary it cannot be the only one.

Performance should have the most important effect on reward after all other factors have been taken into account and compensation should transparently increase in line with the strength of the performance. Here is an example of how that might work:

Performance level	Merit increase percent
1 = poor	0
2 = satisfactory	0
3 = good	3
4 = excellent	4
5 = exceptionally good	5

In practice such straightforward solutions are not always possible but the general thinking should roughly follow these lines. Good performance also affects other benefits, like training and development opportunities within the organisation.

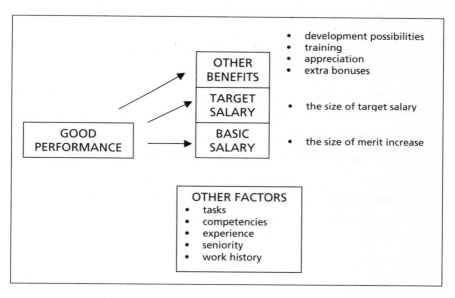

Fig. 2.17   The effect of good performance on rewarding

As discussed earlier, planning and development discussions should not turn into salary discussions. It is sometimes preferable to handle salary matters separately. If they are handled in connection with the planning and development discussion, they can dominate. The subordinate might not wait for anything else except the discussion on the salary. In this case the actual purpose, the planning and development of operations, will disappear into the background.

Career planning

Every now and then the long-term plans of the subordinate should be dealt with in the planning and development discussions. That means not just looking at career plans but thinking about future tasks in the context of the employee's own ambitions and the company's specific needs.

The organisation generally gathers this kind of information and uses it when making succession and career plans. The more systematically these things have been handled in the planning and development discussions, the easier it is to make summaries on the organisation level.

Summary and critical success factors

The aim of performance management is the continuous improvement of performance. That can be connected to the development of customer satisfaction, operative efficiency, overall competence or general well-being. The process of performance management is built on daily leadership, planning meetings and planning and development discussions. The process consists of four basic functions, i.e. objective setting, reviewing/coaching, evaluation of results and development. The performance is examined on an individual, a team and an organisational level. Figure 2.18 shows these basic elements.

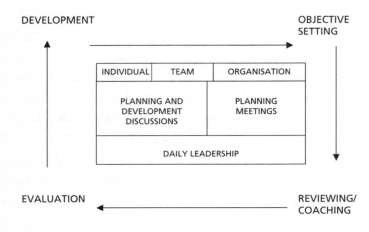

Fig. 2.18   Basic elements of performance management

Joint commitment to the objectives is critical to objective setting. The objectives should also be parallel on an individual, a team and an organisational level. The purpose, key duties and objectives must be clear on all levels. Good objective setting creates positive expectations and energises the organisation.

Reviewing/coaching means, in essence, holding dialogues. It means continuous guidance and feedback, listening and, if necessary, immediate corrective measures. Two-way communication has to be built on trust.

The evaluation of results means making an assessment of the whole. We must stop for a while from time to time to see where we are going. Have we reached our targets? Can we be satisfied with our performance as a whole? It is all about structured feedback and looking at things in their entirety.

Performance management should primarily be directed at the development of performance. It should be forward-looking. How can we be still better? And it should have a determinedly long-term perspective.

So why is it that performance management systems generally do not work very well in organisations? Performance management is not a new thing. There is plenty of experience in its practical implementation, too. Well, one very important reason the process often doesn't work properly is that performance management, especially planning and development discussions, are used as separate tools. They have not been closely linked to the organisation's other management systems. It requires a clarity and breadth across the organisation as a whole, looking at:

- the purpose of the activities;
- the key task areas;
- the objectives; and
- the competence needed.

All the different levels of the organisation need to understand this and communicate with each other. Only then will performance management start to work in practice. Figure 2.19 shows the links and practice of performance management.

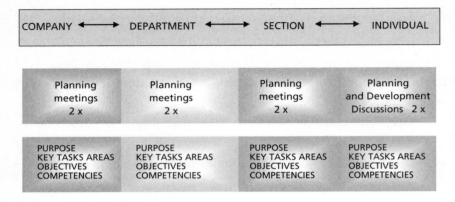

Fig. 2.19 Links and practice of performance management

Sometimes there are situations where a lot is invested in performance management on an individual level. Planning and development discussions get started very well. But the management, despite supporting the implementation of the process as a whole, does not function very well. The necessary connections often aren't made on a department or team level. And middle management becomes a bottle-neck for the development of performance.

Ten critical success factors

Ten critical factors for making a performance management system a success are listed below.

1   It must be simple and easy to use. Keep the KISS principle in mind when building it. (Keep it simple, stupid.)
2   It is integrated to other company processes and human resource management processes.
3   It takes the requirements of the virtual and network organisation into consideration. It can be used to manage performance in a process organisation.

4 Performance management is examined on an individual, a team and an organisational level. Because we work more and more in teams, performance management must also work on a team level.

5 The value discussion of the organisation is important in performance management.

6 It is a continuous process consisting of daily leadership, planning meetings and planning and development discussions.

7 Line managers are the owners of the process. The task of the personnel function is to support the project.

8 The subordinates and superiors have shared responsibility for the working process. It can also be used to manage oneself.

9 It is targeted to the improvement of performance and the development of competencies and mainly to the future.

10 Performance management is linked to competence and knowledge management.

These success factors steered our working when we revised the performance management system at Nokia Telecommunications in 1995. At that time I had responsibility for the performance management project group. Our most important challenges were:

- the many different systems in use;
- systems were considered too complicated and difficult to understand;
- the viewpoint of process management had not been taken into consideration;
- team work and team objectives were not emphasised enough;
- value discussion was not connected to planning and development discussions; and
- planning and development discussions were not clearly a 'top down' process in all units.

We managed to build a new global performance management system in early 1995. We did it with a small (six people) project team covering a wide range of expertise. We succeeded in taking it into use globally during the same year. In addition to the above mentioned 10 success factors, two other factors made a big contribution to our success. Matti Alahuhta, who was CEO at that time, strongly supported the development and implementation of the new performance management system. He referred particularly to the development work and was one of the first users of the new tool. Another factor in our success was that we organised a training session for area and country managers in order to discuss the principles of the new system with them in detail. We wanted to make sure that we had their support for the new system. The use of the system was, of course, also supported by more expanded training.

A couple of years earlier I had been involved in a similar project at Kone Corporation where we built a new performance management system with the help of external consultants. The basic principles of Kone's system was exactly the same. It was also theoretically attractive but just didn't work in practice. In my opinion, this was mainly down to two factors. The global corporate culture was not ready for the introduction of such a tool and the top management was not supportive enough. The episode served to show that the most critical factor is not always the tool itself but successful implementation.

Self-evaluation of the performance management process

You can evaluate the level of performance management in your own organisation by answering the attached 35 statements. Think about how it works in your own organisation. By going through these statements you can perhaps find some areas for improvement.

The questionnaire is divided into the following sections:

1   performance management – general;
2   daily leadership/coaching;
3   planning meetings;
4   evaluation of the results;
5   agreeing on objectives;

6   development plan; and

7   rewarding.

Evaluate each thesis with the following scale: 1 = disagree strongly, 2 = disagree, 3 = difficult to say, 4 = agree, 5 = agree strongly.

General

1   I understand the general principles of performance management.

2   Our organisation has a clearly distinguished process for performance management consisting of planning meetings, planning and development discussions and daily leadership.

3   The management of the company implements the process in an exemplary manner.

4   My own superior implements development discussions regularly and values them.

5   I have received enough training for the planning and development discussions.

Daily leadership/coaching

1   I receive enough feedback from my superior.

2   I have open and confidential relations with my superior.

3   If necessary, I get support from my superior.

4   My superior's management style is distinct, fair and goal-directed.

5   Cooperation is the bread and butter of my department.

Planning meetings

1   Periodic planning meetings are held at my department twice a year.

2   In my opinion I have sufficient opportunity to influence these plans.

3   Planning meetings help me to better understand the objectives of our department/team and connect my own objectives to them.

4   In the planning meetings we can look at things from a new viewpoint and they are not only repetition of what was done before.

5   Planning meetings result in a clear action plan, the implementation of which follows.

The evaluation of results

1   Our organisation has a fair system for performance evaluation.
2   I understand well how the evaluation process of my own performance is working.
3   My superior makes a fair and just performance evaluation.
4   I get enough feedback about my performance.
5   Poor performance is not accepted in our organisation and immediate measures are taken to correct it.

Agreeing on the objectives

1   In my opinion I know well enough the objectives of our organisation and can connect my own objectives to them.
2   I have clear key task areas and key objectives defined on the basis of the key task areas.
3   My own objectives are:
    • concrete;
    • measurable;
    • achievable;
    • meaningful; and
    • time-bound.
4   I have defined my objectives together with my superior.
5   I am also familiar with the other expectations of my superior/my team concerning my work.

Development plan

1   I have an updated personal development plan.
2   I know what kind of competencies are required in my present job.
3   I have a feeling that I can continuously develop my competencies and thus improve my performance.
4   I have the opportunity to discuss my long-term career plans with my superior.
5   I invest personally in the development of my competencies.

Rewarding

1 I have enough information on the salary policy and benefits of our company.
2 I feel good performance affects rewarding.
3 The connection of planning and development discussions to rewarding has been defined in our organisation.
4 Good performance is better rewarded than average performance.
5 Our rewarding system motivates people to work hard and try their best.

I hope that these 35 statements provide a concrete summary of the situation in your own organisation. What are the strengths and where are the weaknesses of the performance management process of your own organisation? The statements that have received the grade 1–3 are probably the most important development areas of your organisation. Consider what the three most urgent development areas and what would be the possible benefits, if these were implemented.

Chapter 3
Competence Management

'Some people are more talented than others. Some are more educationally privileged than others. But we all have capacity to be great. Greatness comes with recognising that your potential is limited only by how you choose.'

Peter Koestenbaum

Continuous improvement of competence as an objective

Competence management process

The competence management process aims at continuously improving competencies so that the organisation is capable of persistent high performance. The process starts with the organisation's vision, strategy and objectives. This is really the only new thing in competence management: a distinct definition of competence in the precise context of the company's strategy. Everything else connected to competence development has already been done earlier by training and development experts. Figure 3.1 shows the framework of competence management.

The process starts with the definition of the organisation's vision, strategy and objectives. We have to ask about the purpose of the organisation and what kind of competence it needs to reach its aims. This is when we determine the core competence of the organisation, something that gives us competitive advantage. Then we divide it into concrete competence areas and competencies on the different levels of the organisation.

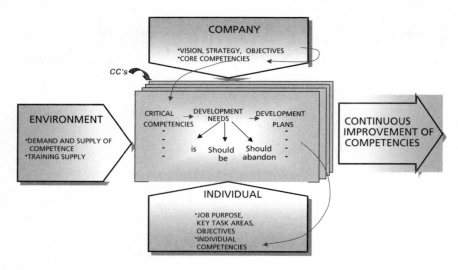

Fig. 3.1 The framework of competence management

Concrete competencies are located in those parts of the company that constitute its particular expertise, which we call competence centres. Today a company can be described as an amalgamation of **competence centres** providing the necessary resources for processes and projects. In practice, one of these centres corresponds to a single department. It can be the technical planning department or the finance department. You can then drill down even further to establish competencies on an individual level. But even these competencies, at this granular level, constitute core competence.

On a competence centre level we define the critical competence that is key to the operation of the department in question. In general this is done by the department manager together with some of his closest subordinates who are well acquainted with the operations of the department. It is important to concentrate on critical competence only, because competence lists will get too long otherwise. Development needs are analysed by defining what kind of competence we have, what we should have, and what we should abandon. We must examine the present situation as well as considering what sort of competence we might need in the next two or three years. The summary of this phase is presented in the development plan of a competence centre that describes how we are going to develop competence during the coming year.

The next phase is the implementation of the development plans on an individual level. Individuals take care of certain tasks, including certain key task areas and objectives. An individual needs certain competencies to cope with his/her duties. At this stage the development plans of the competence centre and the individual plans of the people working there need to be linked to each other. In practice, this happens as part of the planning and development discussions, as if we need reminding how important they are to the functioning of the organisation.

It is important to define the demand and supply of competence as well as the general training supply. By evaluating these factors the organisation can define its own competence, i.e. how it is going to reach the competence level required now and in the future. The improvement of competence within an organisation is, of course, achieved by other means than just training, like recruitment, job rotation, partnerships and sometimes even mergers and acquisitions.

One special characteristic of the competence management approach is that we examine competence against the backdrop of the organisation's vision, strategy and objectives. There are also other more traditional approaches to the improvement of competence, for example:

- traditional surveying methods of training needs;
- job-related competence profiles; and
- competence classifications and listings.

Many books have been written about all this and most organisations have experience of them too. These experiences, in turn, help form the different approaches to competence management and help determine the most effective techniques. But competence management is a new approach, offering a comprehensive way of developing the organisation's human capital in the context of its strategy.

Once competence has been defined, listed and classified, the next question is how and where to store the data. Lots of competence information systems have been developed for this precise purpose. There are off-the-shelf solutions, although some organisations have preferred to develop their own applications. As far as training and development is concerned, this type of software includes the essential data about education, job history, qualifications, multi-field know-how and development plans, and it certainly makes practical work much easier.

Levels of competence

Figure 3.2 helps to simplify some of the concepts connected to competence management. It shows the three dimensions that we need to touch on when we talk about competence. They are:

- organisation level;
- present situation versus future; and
- content of competence.

The concepts of individual competence, competence on the job, team competence, department competence or organisational competence are all totally different. Equally, the present competence level might differ completely from the future competence level. And core competence, process competence, functional competence and general competence are also distinct units.

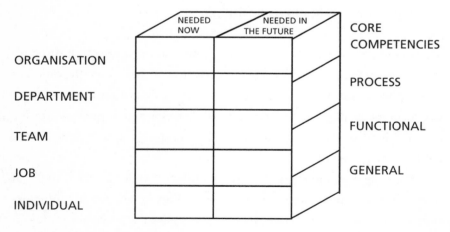

Fig. 3.2 The levels of competence

It is always helpful to define competence and the point of view from which we are analysing it so that we avoid getting these different parts muddled. The biggest obstacle to implementing effective competence management has been some sort of misunderstanding at this level.

Strategic management focuses on competence strategies

Competence management starts with the company's strategy, vision and objectives. You can't define core competence without them. So what is strategy? The word strategy means the road ahead and describes how an organisation is trying to achieve its goals. Vision, again, is an image of the company's future. The company vision should be realistic and well founded and not illusory. Strategy combines the present state with this vision of the future. It is simply one route from the present in the direction of our vision.

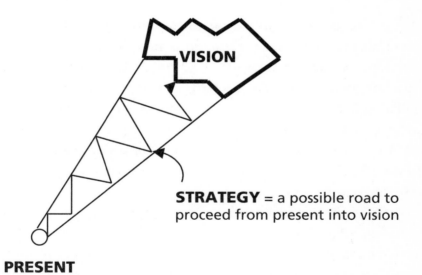

STRATEGY = a possible road to proceed from present into vision

PRESENT

Fig. 3.3 Strategy and vision

For some reason strategy is often experienced as something vague and mysterious. Cynics say strategy is everything that is badly defined and poorly understood. It has been accused of being elitist. 'Strategic matters' used to be the privilege of the organisation's top management. But that has changed in many of today's companies and it is often more inclusive.

Business strategy is a summary of what the organisation wants to be, where it wants to go and how it is going to get there. It asks where we are in our business and how we can make money in that business. It helps position the company within the market with the ambition of achieving a permanent competitive advantage. Strategic management is a continuous process that starts with the drafting of the strategy, moves through strategic planning, implementation and evaluation before beginning the process again. The company's strategy is traditionally revised yearly and the time span of strategic planning is generally 3–5 years. Some IT companies, like Nokia, have moved over to continuous strategic planning updated every six months.

Strategic human resource management

Whereas business strategy defines the general direction and objectives for the organisation, human resource strategy defines what kind of human resources the company needs in order to achieve the targets set. Human resource strategy must, of course, be based on the general strategy, but it can also influence the wider strategy of the company. Staff have become such important stakeholders that human resource strategy has to now include some kind of vision from the perspective of this broader community. This is why Fig. 3.4 shows a two-way arrow between the business strategy and the human resource strategy.

Strategic human resource management means that the human resource function knows the contents of Fig. 3.4. It knows the business strategy of the company as well as its vision and objectives. They build their human resource strategy on this basis. It deals with a wide range of HR issues, from the number of staff, their quality, location, outsourcing, competence, to more abstract issues like motivation. The development of this kind of strategic view is very important for the personnel function and it is dangerous to limit it to just being a practical implementor. It should be an active

Fig. 3.4   Strategic human resource management

partner of the management particularly in defining the strategy, because competent and motivated personnel is vitally important today.

Towards new strategic thinking

During the last ten years strategic thinking has changed considerably and there is a broad church of opinion on the subject. Michael Porter, for example, warns against mixing up operational efficiency and strategy. He says a lot of people don't see the difference between these two. The search for productivity, quality and speed has brought with it a wealth of new management techniques, like quality management, process management, outsourcing, benchmarking, change management, which have brought about considerable operative improvements. But most companies have still not been able to achieve their aim of permanent profits and Porter argues that new management methods have taken the place of the strategy. He says basic strategies – cost leadership, differentiation and focus – are still convenient ways to illustrate the strategic position of the company.

Gary Hamel represents a more distinctly new way of thinking. He says, 'Strategy is revolution, everything else is tactics.' His main target is traditional strategic planning, which he says is just a ritual of the top management. The problem is that we are too often incapable of distinguishing planning from strategy. Planning implemented on the basis of old-fashioned rules will not produce a strategy, he warns. Building a strategy requires a bit more imagination. That is why he recommends that strategic management should involve larger groups of employees. Hamel divides companies into three types: **rule makers** who set the pace, **rule followers** who try to follow the rules, and **rule breakers** who try to change the rules of the industry completely.

In his new book 'Leading the revolution' Hamel says that successful firms will have to go even further than just perfecting organisational learning and knowledge management, which are really just relations of continuous improvement and not the ultimate ambition of innovation and novelty. 'They are more about getting things better than getting different. The final accomplishment of the age of progress was to turn knowledge into a commodity. Today you can buy knowledge by the pound from consultants hawking best practice, from the staff you've just hired from your competitor, and from all those companies that hope you'll outsource everything. Yet in the age of revolution it is not knowledge that produces new wealth, but insight into opportunities for discontinuous innovation. Discovery is the journey; insight is the destination. You must become your own seer.'

Robert S. Kaplan and David P. Norton developed a so-called 'balanced scorecard' that became very popular in the late 1990s. Although not originally developed as a new strategic management technique, that's what it has become. Their balanced scorecard examines the implementation of the strategy from four different viewpoints: the financial viewpoint, the viewpoint of internal business processes, the customers' viewpoint, and a viewpoint of learning and growth (see fig. 3.5). It sees a much wider perspective than just financial figures and is better able to predict the right future action. The weakness of this system, however, is that it does not recognise independently the viewpoint of the wider staff. Their perspective is bundled in with learning and growth but does not, in my opinion, get enough attention there.

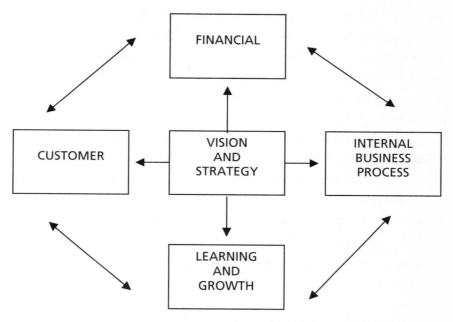

Fig. 3.5 Balanced scorecard: The four viewpoints in the implementation of vision and strategy

Kaplan and Norton say that some companies have started to use a balanced scorecard as a cornerstone of the new strategic management system as a way of replacing traditional management systems and connecting the long-term strategy of the company to the short-term measures.

Kamensky (2000) chronicles the development phases of strategic management as follows: long-term planning (1960s and 1970s), strategic planning (1970s and 1980s), strategic management (1980s and 1990s), strategic thinking and behaviour (1990s and 2000s). He continues this development chain until the 2000s using the concept of **management by interaction** – a management philosophy and way of recognising the ability to see, understand, develop and manage the ever more complex interactive relationships as the key success factor in the strategic management of a company. This network of interactive relationships is built around three concepts: environment, enterprise and the individual. Management by interaction emphasises the fact that all employees participate in the strategic management process. Everyone has an important role to play and their interpersonal skills will go a long way in determining their effectiveness.

Kamensky ends his book saying: 'It is difficult to imagine balanced individual life without the harmony of the missions of both the enterprise and the individual. The circle of strategic management will close here: the strategies of the enterprise and the individuals must be in harmonious interaction with each other.' It is a significant step forward that strategy consultants now identify the role of the individual as being so important. It is also telling that Jagdish Parikh, a leading self-management consultant, concentrates in his last book on management by interaction (Managing Relationships, 1999). Starting from the individual perspective often has the effect of emphasising the importance of different relationships and exposing wider inter-dependencies. It is my belief that this approach, focusing on interaction and relationships, will be a central part of the way we operate in the decade ahead.

Competence strategies

Competence and knowledge are such important success factors that we have developed specific competence or capability strategies. Competence strategies aim to enhance competitive advantage by developing competencies, processes and information systems. It means analysing and developing competence systematically on an individual, team and organisational level. This transformation of traditional strategy into competence strategies is described in Fig. 3.6. In the 70s and 80s, Porterism was the dominant philosophy, basing strategy on cost-leadership, differentiation and focus. In the 90s strategy was replaced by different kinds of management systems aimed more precisely at improving operations. Some of the competence and capability strategies that will be employed in the years ahead also surfaced during the 90s. Figure 3.6 shows the most popular management discipline during each of the periods in question. But it does not mean that the theories that dominated the previous phase were immediately abandoned once we moved on a stage. The key message here is to see how management focus has changed. Today the most important function of the management is to acquire, maintain and develop the competence of the organisation.

1980s	1990s	2000s
TRADITIONAL STRATEGY ⟹	**MANAGEMENT SYSTEMS** ⟹	**COMPETENCE STRATEGIES**
Cost efficiency differentiation focus (Porter)	Lean management process management quality management etc. => continuous improvement of operations and efficiency	Core competencies capability strategies =>management's most important task is to recruit, maintain and develop the competence of the organisation

Fig. 3.6 Strategies focusing on competencies

Core competence as a framework

The most influential book in the sphere of competence management in the 90s was 'Competing for the Future' (1994) by Hamel and Prahalad. The book introduced a framework for the core competence concept and explained how to develop core competencies. The only really new feature in the framework was the idea that the development of competence starts with defining the vision, strategy and objectives of the organisation. After that core competencies are defined both in the context of present needs and future requirements. Once these have been identified, you can move onto defining the appropriate core competencies at the different levels of the organisation.

Definitions of core competencies

Core competence is a combination of competencies, technologies and information systems that make the company competitive. It is a concept that is generally only used on an organisational level. It is made up of accumulated competence that the organisation can exploit in its present or future to give added value to the customer. It should be so deeply embedded in the organisation that it is difficult for competitors to copy and helps the company to develop new products. Core competencies are generally restricted from five to ten areas. There are plenty of other attributes that make a company competitive but core competencies lie at the very heart of its success.

It is often quite difficult to define core competencies. It demands profound knowledge of the organisation. Hamel and Prahalad have defined three ways to test whether something really is a core competence. They ask:

- Does it have any significant influence on the value added for the customer?
- Can it be used to increase the company's competitiveness?
- Can it be applied in other business transactions?

If the answer to all these questions is yes, it most probably is a question of organisational core competence. Here are the key features of core competencies:

- numerically few, restricted to 5–10;
- bring the organisation unique competitive edge;
- bring the customer true value added;
- difficult to copy;
- development takes 3–5 years;
- combination of knowledge, skills, technologies, processes and methods; and
- are born through the cumulative learning process of the organisation.

The company must be seen not only as a portfolio of products and services, but also as that of competencies. Hamel and Prahalad's vision is represented in Fig. 3.7.

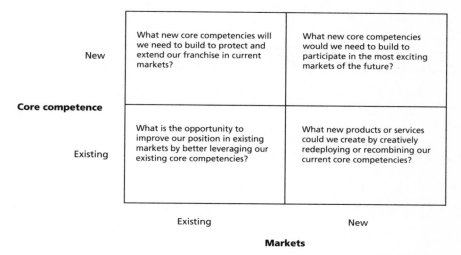

Fig. 3.7 Establishing the core competence agenda according to Hamel and Prahalad

One of the challenges here is establishing how best to implement plans to develop core competence. It isn't easy because the idea of core competence offers only a general framework and not a concrete model. To address this problem we need a detailed definition of the architecture of organisational competence.

Architecture of organisational competence

Organisational competence is made up of core competence and other competence. Core competence creates and maintains the competitiveness of the company. Other competence is also indispensable but it is not unique. Core competence is often a rather general, abstract entity divided into separate competence areas and it is usually a combination of technologies and processes. Competence areas consist of smaller units of tools, methods and sub-processes and they can be divided into concrete competencies. Figure 3.8 shows the competence architecture of the organisation.

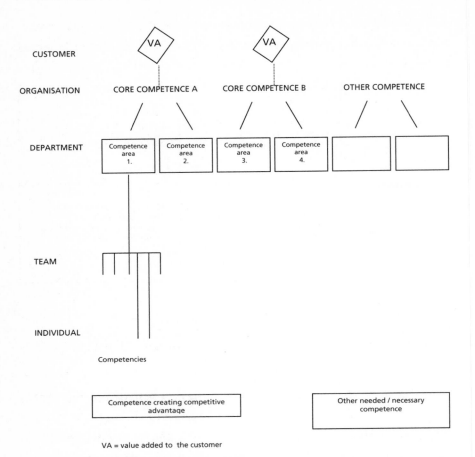

Fig. 3.8 The competence architecture of the organisation

Competence is defined in different ways on different levels. On an individual level it is very concrete. Individual competence includes all knowledge, skills, attitudes, experiences and contact networks. On a more general level, we can define competence as an ability and willingness to perform well in a certain job. On a team level, competence consists of the competencies of the individuals working in that team and of the different combinations of these competencies. On a department level competence is more general and consists of larger areas of expertise but we can still make development plans, because competence is still concrete enough to be connected with the individual level. On a company level competence is defined very generally and is normally fairly abstract. And this is where we talk about core competence. We need to be able to define what kind of added value it brings to the customer. The following are examples of where the core competence concept has been made more concrete.

Nokia's core competencies

Nokia started the core competence project in 1995. We began with the idea that the competitiveness of a company in the long term depends on its ability always to create new products and services bringing excellent value added to its customers. Core competencies were defined so that we could understand, systematically exploit and develop the competence that was the supporting pillar of the company's competitiveness. Eight core competencies were identified by the project. These key areas are shown in Fig. 3.9. At the early stage Nokia concentrated merely on technical competence.

Digital signal processing
Usability
Radio technology
Telecommunications software platforms and architectures
Mastering telecommunications networks
Fast creation of systems and products to selective market needs
Electronics manufacturing
Global customer service

Fig. 3.9   The core competencies of Nokia

Core competencies are the result of the cumulative learning process of the organisation and are divided into competence areas in the different parts of the organisation. Competence areas are further drilled down into competencies that can be defined as the ability of the individuals to perform certain tasks. Figure 3.10 shows an example on how the core competence 'Mastering Telecommunications Networks' is divided into competence areas and competencies.

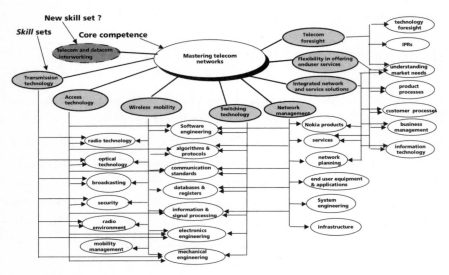

Fig. 3.10 Dividing the core competence 'Mastering Telecommunications Networks' into competence areas and competencies

Each core competence area had a mentor, assistant and project group consisting of experts from different parts of Nokia. The target of the project group was to define, maintain, co-ordinate and develop the competencies in this core competence area. The project was started by the Nokia Research Centre and led by the steering group of the core competence project.

In addition to defining core competencies the localisation of competence in the organisation, its co-ordination and systematic development was an essential part of the project. Moreover, this project aimed at making the employees more conscious of the importance of the proactive development of competence and at making sure that each business unit would start systematic development on the basis of the core competence concept. The project was a big investment in the development of competence at Nokia. At the end of the 1990s it became more concrete and is now effectively implemented in different business units. Today Nokia does not use the core competence concept any more but it was a necessary and instructive development phase that supported the organisational learning process. Now we are trying to look for new methods that work still better in continuous and fast change.

Core competencies of the Finnish Broadcasting Company (YLE)

At the start of the new millennium the Finnish Broadcasting Company (YLE) is making a big investment in the maintenance and development of competence. It wants to embed competence management into the fabric of the organisation so that the critical know-how needed to be successful is available now and in the future. The different branches and units are splitting the competence areas into more detailed parts and further into tasks and knowledge and skills needed in these tasks. The corporate core competence areas are based on the corporate strategy and broadcasting legislation. Figure 3.11 shows the core competence of YLE divided into three parts: programmes and contents, technology and YLE's common core competence.

PROGRAMMES AND CONTENTS	COMMON YLE CORE	TECHNOLOGY
• Programme planning • Programme production • Journalistic competence • Story-telling • Transmission of events/experiences • Production and layout of the contents of the network services	• YLE management • YLE-spirit	• Media technology • Data systems management • Techno-economic competence

Fig. 3.11   Core competence areas of YLE

At YLE the definition of core competencies was the starting point of building a concrete competence model of the key requirements for different task groups on a corporate level. The competence model is also used to create recruitment criteria and to clarify the contents of development discussions. It provides a framework for the long-term development of the personnel and helps them to see the relationship between the strategic objectives and competence available in the company. Figure 3.12 shows the framework of the competence model of YLE.

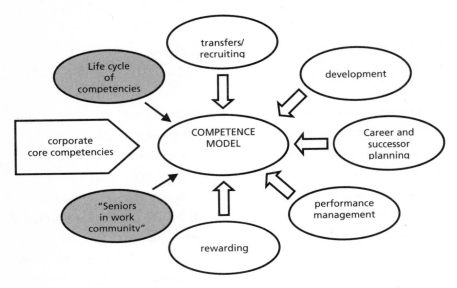

Fig. 3.12 The competence model of YLE (the Finnish Broadcasting Company)

How to develop core competencies

Because the development of organisational core competence is so important we are going to take a look at how to support it with competence, performance and knowledge management. On a corporate level, core competence is the combination of competencies and technologies that enable successful competition. Core competencies can be divided into competence areas and these further into competencies. Concrete competence (know-how) works on the individual level. Employees have competence that is part of some competence area. The lower the level we are looking at, the more concrete is the competence.

Organisations are often good at defining visions and strategies. The problem is how to communicate these to the staff and put them into practice. The competence management process incorporates some elements of strategic management because it communicates the competence strategy through different units, departments and teams to the individual. It shows us the path from the vision of the organisation into concrete development activities on the individual level.

Performance management on an individual level means that the employee is able to give a direct answer to the following four questions:

- What is the meaning of my job?
- What are my most important tasks?
- What are my key objectives?
- What kind of competence do I need in order to be able to perform well?

Individual competence is measured against the present job but also considers the changes caused by the company's long-term strategy.

The development of the competence of the staff always starts from the development of individual competence. An individual learns something, implements it and shares his/her competence with his/her team. In order to exploit our competence better we must document what we have learnt. One way of doing this is to draft working instructions. With these instructions we create a new practice which will be implemented at the departmental level as well as in other units as official practice. It also takes the hidden knowledge of an individual or a team and makes it available to the whole organisation. If this competence brings a truly competitive edge to the organisation, we can say that the company has created new core competence. Figure 3.13 shows how we can support the development of core competencies by competence, performance and knowledge management.

Competence management in practice

In practice, competence management means that we must at first crystallise the organisation's vision, strategy and objectives. After that we must define the core competencies that bring significant competitive edge to the company and added value to the customer. The definition of these core competencies is not always easy to do for the first time. It is, however, an interesting process that requires the management to think through organisational competence and its

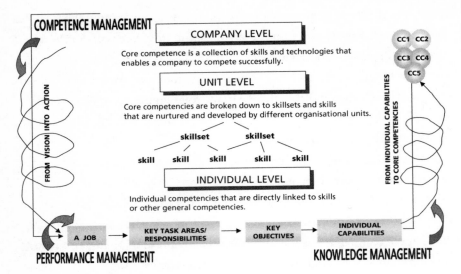

Fig. 3.13 How to develop core competencies

significance as a competitive factor. It is also normally the starting point of the definition and development process of competence in the organisation.

In practice, competence management is working on many levels simultaneously. Bigger organisations normally include the following levels:

- company/organisation;
- division;
- (business) unit;
- department (competence centre);
- team; and
- individual.

The idea of competence becomes more abstract the higher we move up the organisation. This is why we often feel that core competence is such an abstract idea that it is actually unhelpful. So it is good to understand the logic dividing core competencies into different competence areas and further into concrete competencies. Competence management is often implemented as a 'top to bottom' process, defining core competencies first before considering which of them are already represented across the different levels of the organisation. The next step is to implement the process on the 'bottom to top' principle. That means looking at the individual competence level, how it adds up on the team, departmental, unit, and corporate levels. It is that approach that often throws up something new or exposes a weakness. We probably need numerous top to bottom processes and bottom to top processes before core competencies will be crystallised and have a really significant role in the development of organisational competence on different levels.

Figure 3.14 visualises competence management in practice. It works on different levels as an interactive process. The concrete definition of competencies takes place on a department or competence centre level. I found this the biggest insight when implementing competence management over the last five years. Each department in the organisation must have some concrete competence bringing added value to the whole organisation. One of the major tasks of the department manager is to maintain and continuously develop that competence. He also needs to see how this competence supports the implementation of the strategy and visions of the whole organisation. He must also take care that the plans to develop departmental competence feed through the performance management process, with the help of the planning and development discussions, into individual development plans. That's why the department managers are the main owners of the process.

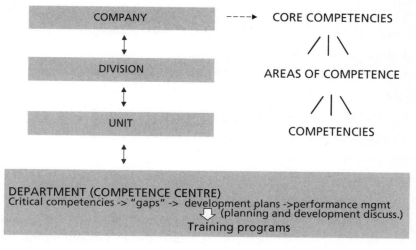

Fig. 3.14 Competence management in practice

Critical competencies are defined inside the department and concrete development plans are drafted on the basis of competence gaps for the coming year. These plans steer the development of the team or individual alongside development discussions. These plans can also be used in the planning process of traning programmes and they give guidelines for training budgeting.

Below you will find three examples of competence management in practice. The first example is the presentation of a competence development process at Nokia. The second example looks at how the training unit of this same division defined the basic services and competencies it required. The third example is ICL Finland. This example shows how they have implemented competence management during the last few years. The idea is for these examples to make the competence management appear more concrete.

The competence development process of one division at Nokia

When Nokia adopted the core competence concept in 1996, we started its implementation in our own division. At the time we had about 3,000 employees globally and product development centres spread around the world. The implementation of a systematic competence management process was a serious challenge.

Our target was to create a very simple process that we could benefit from immediately and that could be implemented globally. Our organisation at the time was divided into approximately 50 competence centres. The major role in this exercise was played by the managers of these different departments. We sent them a very short 'concrete version' of the competence management process. The package consisted of one written sheet of paper, one transparency and some software that helped set up the competence management process. We figured that by keeping it extremely simple and clear we could start things move more easily and clearly demonstrate the benefits. Later on the process can get more complicated if necessary.

Figure 3.15 shows what competence management meant at Nokia (our division) in practice. Each department manager thought about the corporate vision, strategy and objectives and what they meant to their own

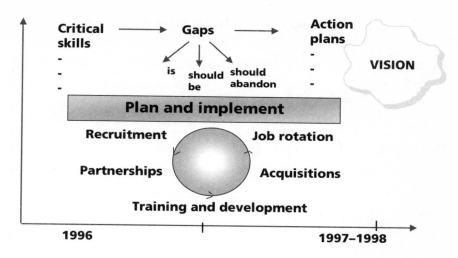

Fig. 3.15 An example of competence management in practice

department. They asked themselves exactly what competencies they needed to fulfil those objectives at that level. They were also required to define their development needs and they were asked to think about what kind of competence they could afford to abandon – something very often overlooked. The exercise of answering all these questions produced the material that went into the departmental development plans.

The development plan of the department was made with the tool presented in Fig. 3.16, listing:

- the most important competencies (generally 5–15);
- present strength and target strength on a three-step scale;
- objective for each competence defined;
- very concrete development plan for the next year; and
- more general development plan in the long term.

Some departments found the exercise straightforward. Others needed a lot of support.

There are a few basic principles in making the development plan. First of all we must concentrate on critical competence that really is of vital importance for the operations of the department. If there are too many compe-

Competence Development Plan

Strengths: 3=very strong, 2=strong, 1=weak

name
competence centre
date

CRITICAL COMPETENCIES	Current strength/ strength target (1–3)	Number of masters/ target	Objective for this competence area	ACTION PLAN 1996–98 Training and development	ACTION PLAN 1997–1998 Training and development

Fig. 3.16   Competence development plan

tencies, they don't focus action. This is why 5–15 competencies is generally a good number. We started by defining our critical technical competencies. It is always worth bearing in mind that this can take a while to develop.

Secondly, the objectives for every competence must be defined concretely and the resulting development plan for the next year must be practical. It should list deadlines and responsibilities for each measure. That makes it easier to adapt them to individual employee development plans. Figure 3.17 shows an example of the competence development plan of the human resources department.

When our division did this exercise for the first time, involving about 50 different departments, we came up with almost 500 critical competencies altogether. Some departments had defined nearly all their competencies and there were some overlapping areas. So we sent a summary of the results as feedback to the department managers and gave some instructions for the next time. This way the number of competencies and competence areas was reduced and we began to find the critical competencies that could bring our division true competitive advantage. After a few rounds, the division had

COMPETENCE AREAS AND DEVELOPMENT PLANS OF HR DEPARTMENT			
COMPETENCE AREA/ CRITICAL SKILLS	LEVEL present/ target	OBJECTIVES IN THIS AREA	PLAN OF ACTION -99
PRODUCT COMPETENCE	1/2	Basic understanding of our key products in order to be able to analyse present and future competencies.	Participation in product training whenever possible.
HUMAN RESOURCES PLANNING	1/3	Better understanding of telecommunication business and deeper understanding of BBS vision and strategies. Ability to connect business strategy and HRM strategy.	BBS vision and strategy communicated to all and discussed with Jaakko Saijonmaa 9/99 PkS
ORGANISATIONAL LEARNING RECRUITMENT	2/3	Better understanding of: Performance management	IIP training can be offered by PkS, AK, MPe, AS, LeL
		Competence management	Competence management support can be given by PkS, AK, MPe, AS, LeL
		Knowledge management	Acquire basic understanding about knowledge management in practice.
		Team management	Teamframe concept understood and implemented.
		Change management	Implementation of CoAch project
HUMAN RESOURCES DEVELOPMENT	2/3	Widen the abilities to support line organisation in training and induction.	Training and induction support can be offered by HR-consultants. Organise co-operation with Learning Centres
MANAGEMENT DEVELOPMENT	2/3	Ability to give information about NTC management training.	Management training information given by all consultants.
		Ability to use mentoring in management development	Organise some mentoring projects.
SALARY AND EMPLOYMENT MATTERS	2/3	Increase the knowledge about job evaluation systems and variable income systems.	HR-team will be trained 9/99 PkS
HR PROCEDURES AND SYSTEMS	1/3	Ability to use the SAP/R3 applications.	Everybody will participate in the basic training.

Fig. 3.17 Development plan of the human resources department

identified ten competence areas divided into less than a hundred critical and concrete competencies. This listing included mainly technical competencies. On average, ten competencies were also found at the department level and exact development plans were drafted for all of these.

We made competence management plans twice a year, in June and December. In June we made a more detailed report based on the new strategy and in December we updated the plans and examined implementation. It is really important that competence management is connected to the strategy process and that it is repeated frequently. The more familiar people become with the exercise the greater the rewards.

Competence development in the training department

This is an example of how we implement competence management thinking in practice on a department and team level. It describes a four-member training team that is a part of the HR department. The team tries to define:

- what services they should offer;
- what is the 'core competence' of the team, the basis of producing good training services; and
- what is the concrete competence the team needs?

The illustration uses a tree model. The leaves describe the most important basic services of the team. The trunk of the tree is the 'core competence' of the team and the roots are their concrete competencies. The tree model is simple enough and makes the essential points concrete. The most important services of this team have been grouped into the following six areas:

- planning of development and training;
- implementation of courses;
- orientation;
- performance management;
- competence management; and
- learning support systems.

In order to be able to offer good services and added value in the organisation the team must take care that:

- it masters the whole area;
- it practises continuous, systematic development;
- it takes care of customer satisfaction; and
- it evaluates the effectiveness of the training and the team's own results.

The implementation of these things requires many kinds of concrete competence split into knowledge, skills, values, attitudes, contacts and experiences.

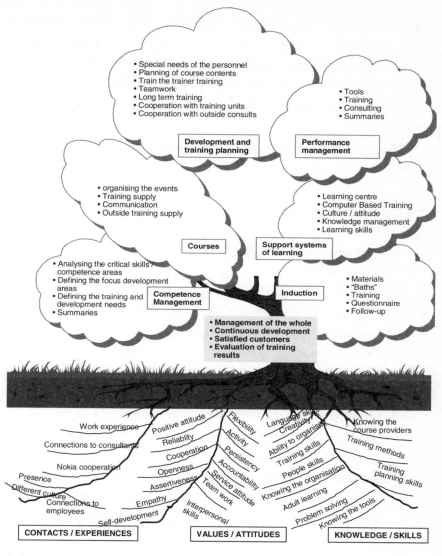

Fig. 3.18 Competencies of the training team

Competence development at ICL Finland

This section describes competence development at ICL Finland during the period 1996–1999. The planning of systematic competence management was started in 1996 by defining the core processes of the business operations and their support processes. In a fast-changing industry, guaranteeing future competence was one of the main drivers of the competence development work. The resourcing of customer projects also needed more measures and tools. The company needed to show customers that it could guarantee the latest competence level at any time during an even longer business relationship.

The competence management process was divided into three different phases:

- management of present competence;
- identification of competence needed in the future; and
- localisation of competence development needs and implementation of development measures.

Simple competence data banks had already been developed for resourcing needs. It was easy to proceed from this basis and start developing a more refined system of managing the present state of competence and build a systematic working method around that. The core of the working method was the target and development discussion. Each ICL employee updated the data about their competence in the Ossi competence system. Discussion with the manager focused on essential targets related to business operations and the competence needed to meet these targets. The manager was also responsible for making subjective competence evaluations of his own staff on as comparable a basis as possible. The Ossi system involved grading competence (split into three parts: general ICL competence, technical competence and business competence) and was used on-line with the help of a web-tool.

The following have been the challenges of managing the present state of competence:

- Motivation of the personnel and managerial staff to maintain and exploit the competence data bank.
- Problems in measuring competence data: can competence be measured and how can we make competence evaluations comparable with each other?

- Building the competence data bank: finding suitable scope and accuracy for the grading.

The identification of future competence needs was mostly based on the views of the managers looking at the business and customer strategies. Each manager decided on the target competence of his/her own subordinates updated in the Ossi system and discussed the competence development needs with them, making a distinction between present and target competence. At this stage there were two potential problems. Firstly, the view of a single manager on the sort of competence that would be needed in the future could be limited. Secondly, the maintenance of the Ossi system as a part of the workload of the superior might be ignored because of more urgent duties.

But lessons were learnt quickly. The development needs of competence and meeting these needs had to be the responsibility of the owners of the competence management process in conjunction with the human resources unit. The owners of the process represented the different business units and had an idea of the needs of their own unit. So, in association with HR, they worked to produce measures to fill perceived skills gaps both on an individual and a corporate level.

In practice, people identified a handful of obstacles in the way of competence development. They were:

- The turnaround time of the competence management process was not always enough for the needs of a dynamic business.
- The measurability of competence was questioned and that made the discussion about competence too abstract.
- The documentation resulting from the competence management process and the maintenance of the system took time, and there was never enough time.

The definition of the competence management process and the work of the process owners in different units as well as the representatives of the human resources unit over the last three years has produced the following results:

- Competence and competence management have indisputably been found to be one of the basic requirements of success in business.
- Both management and personnel feel that the company is investing in competence development and it is appreciated.
- Competence and development have achieved a stable position as a part of the target setting (target and development discussions).
- Competence is developed at ICL in the areas of management and sales as well as in the service and project sectors, and in chosen areas of technical competence.

In order to improve the uniformity of the competence data, ICL established job-specific competence profiles that communicated to people in different functions the essential areas of expertise from their own viewpoint.

In the next phase ICL invested in trying to find the connections between strategy and competence, trying to produce an even tighter definition of target competence. The task was a challenge both on the business unit level and on the corporate level. It started with the questions: What is typical of the industry and what sort of competence provides a competitive edge? What sort of competence is essential as far as strategy is concerned? How does the term core competence fit into the total concept? ICL ended up identifying the strategic competencies that gave them a competitive edge and were important for the implementation of its strategy. But it was not easy to draw the line there. There was plenty of discussion about the strategic significance of certain technical areas of expertise. Could mastering a certain system, for example, be strategic?

The definition of indicators for competence and the competence management process was under consideration throughout the whole project. The firm had been able to measure the level and amount of competence for a long time, but the reporting systems were still unclear.

The final stage was to strengthen the connections between competence management and business management and the continuous follow-up of the chosen strategic competencies. ICL has continued to develop all the ideas that were thrown up during the process but has succeeded in making competence management an integral part of steering the business and not just a separate process.

Individual competence

Competence has become an important means of survival and is the only real employment security for the individual. Today organisations cannot guarantee their employees a continuous and permanent employment. For an individual the only way to guarantee his/her own employment is to take good care of his/her own competence. This defines his/her labour market value. As long as he/she has competence that an organisation is ready to pay for, then he/she is fairly safe. As far as the individual is concerned it would be better, if he/she could detect when the competence was starting to decay or or was heading towards redundancy. When the employer notices that, it might already be too late for the individual.

Psychological employment contract

In a way we are redefining the so-called psychological employment contract. Earlier this was mostly based on trust and mutual loyalty. Today loyalty hardly exists in this respect. The present psychological employment contract is based on competence. The employee assumes that the employer is ready to invest in his/her long-term efforts to develop his/her competence, i.e. to take care of his/her labour market value. In return he/she is committed and loyal to the employer.

The employer, for his part, expects that the employee is committed to continuously maintaining and developing his/her competence. The employer is ready to create a framework for this, but demands a certain amount of initiative and independence from the employee. It is important that both parties understand their own obligations and responsibilities. Only then can this new psychological employment contract work in practice and create a basis for the implementation of a life-long learning principle in practice.

Personal development plan

For the individual, working and regular planning and development discussions are the most important tool in developing his/her competence. Individual competence must be evaluated twice a year and a concrete, personal development plan must be made for him/her. The implementation of the plan must also be followed. Future competence needs should also be examined when making the development plan, alongside some consideration of long-term aims.

It will be a big help in drafting a personal development plan if the organisation has made the necessary competence visible. This means, for example, publicising the most common competence profiles of different jobs. That allows the individual to evaluate his/her own competence and to develop it by measuring it against the different competence profiles.

The existence of a personal development plan is, in fact, a good indicator. It can be used to evaluate how well competence management works in practice. If each employee has a development plan updated twice a year, the company is probably investing enough in competence management and it can also be seen in practice. It should prevent a situation arising where the employee is suddenly found totally unqualified for his/her duties.

Career and successor planning is another tool with which individual competence can be systematically developed in the long term. In most organisations career and succession planning is implemented only for the top management. But we may well ask if intelligent organisations should expand this activity to concern all the employees. But ultimately, an individual always has the main responsibility for their own competence. He/she must also understand this. Everybody is the best manager of his/her own working career that lasts over 40 years and can include many phases. We can use different organisations as an environment to promote our own professional growth, but we must bear the responsibility ourselves. But not all employees are capable of bearing that responsibility. Where that is so the responsibility and ethics of the organisation will be emphasised and an intelligent organisation must accept this obligation.

Summary: what did we learn?

What is most important in competence management? Firstly, it is good to understand some basic concepts of strategic management because it is ultimately going to be based on the implementation of competence strategies. You need to explain to yourself the basic concepts of strategy, particularly if you work in human resources: one of your future roles is to become strategic partner of the management level.

The core competence approach requires thorough and long-term knowledge of the organisation. It can be implemented with the help of consultants, but it is the organisation's own personnel who must do the work. When defining core competencies we are at the core of business operations: we are considering the basic questions connected to the existence of the organisation.

The implementation of competence management is a long process. It is also a process that should be repeated twice every year. It is a learning process. When you do it many times, the results develop and improve all the time. It is also important that competence management is clearly tied to the strategy process and clearly connected to the performance management system. Figure 3.19 illustrates the connections between strategy, competence and performance management processes. Competence management combines the strategy process with the performance management process. It is the tool to implement strategic competence development at an individual level.

In this example (Fig. 3.19) strategy is worked out in February, March and April. When it is completed, strategies and competence plans can be drafted on a departmental level on the basis of the overarching company strategy. Department strategies will be finished during May and June. Competence development plans on the departmental level are a key element of the planning and development discussions that will take place in August. Training and development budgets can be made on the basis of departmental competence development plans firmed up during these discussions. The follow-up and updating of the development plans (December) and another planning and development round (December and January) take place at the end of the year. Furthermore, the competence development plans for the whole organisation should be discussed in the management group, possibly in January. This is how the top management gets involved in the process and familiarises itself with competence issues when starting the strategy process.

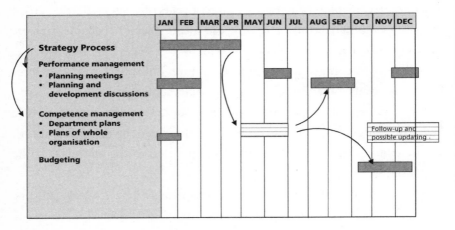

Fig. 3.19   Competence management linked to other processes

It is also very important that we clearly understand the basic concepts connected to competence. We should not get hung up with trendy terms. Make a simple and clear concrete model that you understand yourself and have no problems in selling to the line organisation. Organisations still have a long way to go in this respect; conceptual ambiguity and confusion is a huge problem in competence management.

It is good to remember that line management is responsible for the process of competence management. Very often it is the manager of the competence centre or department, who is responsible. This is his/her tool. The human resource unit is the process maker, mentor and tool developer, but line management must feel that they have the responsibility for the process. When each department makes good competence development plans, it is easy for the training unit to build different training and development programmes around them.

Competence management is a survival issue both on an organisational and an individual level. Seeing it like that should mean that it gets enough attention. It also means that the top management of the organisation gets involved in the definition of core competencies. In an intelligent organisation the most important task of the management is to acquire, maintain and develop organisational competence.

Chapter 4
Knowledge Management

Continuous application of new knowledge as an objective

Knowledge has become an important competitive advantage for organisations. Companies compete for high performers more aggressively than ever before. Lacking competence and knowledge are the most critical factors restricting the development of operations at many hi-tech companies. Knowledge has become significant capital both for companies and their employees. And the significance of knowledge has grown so much, that a new management fad, knowledge management, sprang up during the 1990s.

We face a new challenge. How can we manage the huge amount of knowledge that is available to everybody nowadays? The explosive growth of knowledge has produced a major challenge for us all – how to control the flow so we can analyse the content.

Not knowing what they actually know can be a real problem for organisations. The knowledge needed may be somewhere in the organisation but it is hard to find it. Another problem is that we don't necessarily know what we should know. And the third problem, especially in big organisations, is how to make knowledge available to everybody. Organisations would be much more effective if they only knew what they know. Today we spend a lot of time trying to find knowledge or trying to reinvent things. Knowledge management is one of the keys to making our operations more effective. The knowledge in the organisation must be made visible and available for everybody.

Not all knowledge is important. It must be meaningful and we must be able to use it. The most important objective of knowledge management is the continuous application of new knowledge in practice. **Knowledge management** is a process of creating, capturing, storing, sharing and applying knowledge. In these subprocesses the knowledge of the individual becomes the knowledge of the team and explicit knowledge becomes tacit knowledge. The final objective is the application of knowledge in a decision-making situation because with better knowledge we make better decisions.

For the organisation, it is important that the concept of knowledge management has been clearly defined. As a concept it can be very vague. We try to concretise knowledge management with the help of the following framework (Fig. 4.1). Everything starts, of course, from the strategy and objectives of the organisation, because they determine what kind of knowledge is significant within the organisation. Secondly, the organisation must offer the learning support systems helping us to create, capture, store, share and apply knowledge. And thirdly, the support of human resource management and effective IT systems is important.

As far as the individual is concerned, it is essential that he/she has the ability and willingness to learn new things, to change, to distribute and receive knowledge and, above all, apply it in practice. This also applies to teams. Good teamwork is one of the basic preconditions for knowledge

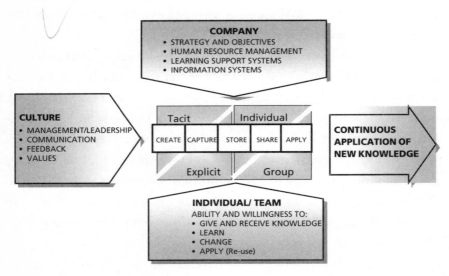

Fig. 4.1   The framework of knowledge management

management. In an organisation the team is often the basic unit of learning and distribution of knowledge. If the distribution of knowledge succeeds well in a team, it most probably succeeds in the whole organisation, too.

In the organisation, it is the culture that creates the framework for knowledge management and its values should support this knowledge sharing. By values, we mean continuous learning, openness and respect for the individual. Empowerment, open and informal communication and generous feedback are also culture-related factors supporting knowledge management.

Starting points for knowledge management

Why did knowledge management become a fad of the 90s? There were many sources of its evolution. The ten most important ones are listed in Fig. 4.2 below.

The most important competitive advantage and capital of the organisation is the knowledge its employees have or the knowledge that is tied to the processes of the organisation. The importance of knowledge as a competitive advantage has become so inescapable that companies are ready to invest in knowledge management. In his book *The 5th Generation Manage-*

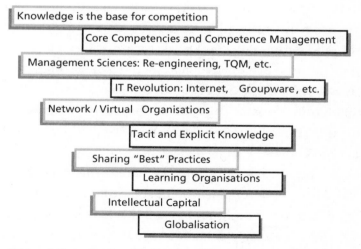

Fig. 4.2   Factors influencing the development of knowledge management

ment Savage presents a diagram where we see how the source of wealth has changed from land to workforce, and further to capital, and today to knowledge (Fig. 4.3).

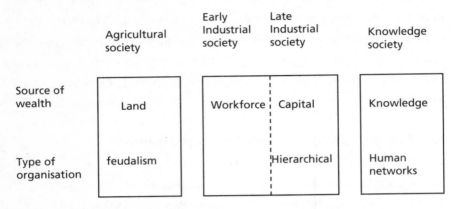

	Agricultural society	Early Industrial society	Late Industrial society	Knowledge society
Source of wealth	Land	Workforce	Capital	Knowledge
Type of organisation	feudalism		Hierarchical	Human networks

Fig. 4.3   The source of wealth and organisation types (source: Savage 1990)

Competence management, another of the big fashions of the 1990s, has also played a role. It is mostly based on the core competence concept of Prahalad and Hamel that they launched in their book *Competing for the Future* (1994). Their approach has contributed a lot to knowledge management. Competence management has perhaps a broader perspective. Knowledge management concentrates more on creating and storing knowledge and on its use in the organisation.

The third starting point for knowledge management is process management. It defines the core and support processes of the company. The objective is to describe the operations of the company as processes that bring added value to the customer. This approach helps us to check whether we are really doing the right things (processes) and doing the things right. Process management is just one view on the systematic collection, storage and distribution of knowledge. People, processes and information technology are the three paths to the development of the knowledge organisation.

The new possibilities enabled by information technology have produced a wealth of new tools for knowledge management. Internet, intranet and groupware-applications offer almost limitless possibilities. It is impor-

tant to remember, however, that information technology only offers tools to control knowledge, but this still opens up a huge array of new working methods and revolutionises earlier ways of working.

Knowledge management is more challenging in new organisational structures. We are moving all the time from traditional organisations towards network and virtual organisations. In virtual organisations people do not sit in the same place or even in the same country. Knowledge, however, must flow fast. Information technology offers many possibilities for the control of the knowledge of these virtual teams. Savage argues, however, that only 10–30% of knowledge that is needed in a company can be stored in the information systems, databases and manuals of the company. The majority of the knowledge needed is in the possession of people working for the company and that is why effective teamwork is so important. And it means heavy investment in teamwork and in the creation of team networks where knowledge flows.

The sixth important starting point for knowledge management is the division of knowledge into explicit and tacit knowledge. Ikujiro Nonaka and Hirotaka Takeuchi are pioneers in this area. In their book *The Knowledge-Creating Company* they present ways to control and exploit the tacit knowledge in the company that has not been documented, and is locked inside the heads of the employees. Understanding the significance of the tacit knowledge within the organisation has been one of the most important new issues in knowledge management.

'The best practices' approach means that we capture information on the processes of the company both from within the company and outside it. This systematic collection of reference information is a key part of knowledge management. However, it should be remembered that the boundaries of the organisation might often be vague in practice and do not have much significance in knowledge management.

We have been talking about a learning organisation for about twenty years, which has helped to prepare for the concept of knowledge management. Knowledge management, in fact, can help concretise elements of the learning organisation, just as competence management deals with some of the same themes. In this respect, knowledge management is sometimes just a label for established concepts. It is more or less the same goods in a new package.

The ninth starting point for knowledge management is to examine the different types of capital within the organisation. Leif Edvinson was one of the first practitioners to identify the intellectual capital of the company. According to him there are four kinds of capital within a company:

- financial capital;
- capital connected to customer relations;
- capital connected to the organisation; and
- capital connected to the employees.

The three last items form the basis of the so-called intellectual capital of the company. The market value of the company consists of financial and intellectual capital. If we speak of the market value of the IT companies, it is the intellectual capital that counts for the majority of the capital. The difference between the book value and market value of a company can be enormous. The majority of this capital is knowledge connected to customer relations, the organisation or employees. Knowledge management self-evidently plays an important role here in supporting the development of all constituents of intellectual capital.

Globalisation has also increased the significance of effective knowledge management. Knowledge should be made available to everyone irrespective of time and place. The fast development of telecommunications technology has made many new applications possible, such as e-mail, company global information networks and video-conferences. Geographical distances have lost their meaning.

What is knowledge management?

The ultimate aim of knowledge management is the effective application of knowledge in decision-making situations. Knowledge itself is not important. It must be meaningful and it must be applicable. Knowledge can be new or old or borrowed; the origin is insignificant. As far as the organisation is concerned, the important thing is that the knowledge is available with fairly little effort and that it can be applied.

Knowledge management as a concept is still fairly undeveloped. The content of the concept also varies a lot. In many organisations knowledge management is banned as a term, because it is considered just a fad. They speak in more everyday and concrete terms which is often a better solution.

The subprocesses of knowledge management

Knowledge management is a process in which knowledge is created, captured, stored, shared and applied. These are the subprocesses of knowledge management. These subprocesses concretely support things like the transformation of quiet knowledge (tacit) into perceptible knowledge (explicit), or individual knowledge into group knowledge. There can be many kinds of processes, procedures and tools within an organisation that are used to manage knowledge. The subprocesses of knowledge management are briefly defined below.

Creation

The creation of new knowledge can happen in many ways. It can be individual studying, brainstorming in a group, work in an interfunctional team, job rotation, etc. Working at the product development department is typically action aiming at creating new knowledge.

Capture (capturing knowledge)

Capturing knowledge means, among other things, participating in a training course, reading books, Internet searches, benchmarking. Knowledge is searched from within the organisation, from other organisations, universities, etc. Capturing knowledge can also be transformation of tacit knowledge into explicit knowledge and the documentation of this knowledge in such a form that it is easily transferred to others.

Because so much knowledge is available, it is important how we look for knowledge. We should be able to quickly get to the knowledge we need. Traditionally this is something that is done by the company's information service. In IT companies it is the role of each employee to search knowledge actively and independently.

Storing

As knowledge increases so the importance of storing it grows. Captured or created knowledge must be further processed into such a form that it is easily available for everybody. This means the handling of knowledge, analysing it and editing it so that the databases of the company are logically organised, reliable and accurate. On an individual level this means reflection and understanding. For this we need time. The individual also needs to keep his/her knowledge stores – internal and external – in good order. If this is not done, knowledge cannot be exploited effectively and it becomes an unhelpful flood of information.

Knowledge is stored in different documents, minutes, memos, manuals and working instructions. The most effective way to store it is in electronic form, which means using database systems.

Sharing

Only shared knowledge is significant for the organisation. Knowledge should be easily available for everybody and good storage is a precondition for effective sharing. There are many different data distribution channels, such as e-mail, mailing of a paper report, Web sites, the use of databases or convening a meeting.

Sharing knowledge requires a company culture that encourages people to share it and to freely exchange their thoughts, ideas and ways of working. Good information systems offer effective tools for sharing. We must not forget, however, the significance of personal contacts, informal networks and traditional communication. This becomes more and more important as the amount of knowledge increases. We need a reliable person to tell us what is significant knowledge.

Application

Ultimately, it is the application of knowledge that benefits the organisation. We should avoid extra work by establishing at the outset what kinds of methods are already used in the organisation before we start trying to invent the wheel again. Usually organisations exploit only a small part of the knowledge they actually have. If knowledge is easily available, it is most probably also exploited. Of course the problem sometimes is that we want to develop our own solutions and not use what already exists.

These subprocesses of knowledge management are concrete processes that the organisation must maintain and develop. The processes must be defined and these ways of working must be employed properly. That way knowledge management becomes a very concrete exercise that can be measured and developed.

In order to work effectively the process of knowledge management requires certain things from the organisation, individual and teams, and from the wider company culture. As far as the company is concerned, the most important thing is the infrastructure that supports the knowledge management process. That means things like human resource management and IT tools. But we need to go further and ask ourselves some basic questions. What do we mean by knowledge management? What is the process of knowledge management and its connections to the other processes of the company? What kind of knowledge management organisation are we creating? Do we need a new position in the company with the title 'Chief Knowledge Officer'? What kind of tools will be used, etc.? The most important thing, of course, is to create a kind of vision of where we are and where we want to be as well as the strategy of knowledge management.

Secondly, the company must consider how the learning support systems relate to the subprocesses of knowledge management. We can, for example, consider how the office space solutions support effective sharing of knowledge. Sometimes a coffee machine helps a lot in the sharing of knowledge, even if it was not originally developed for this purpose. People tend to gather around it at regular intervals to chat. And the processes of human resource management should support knowledge management. Sometimes different kinds of rewarding methods are needed for knowledge management purposes, since people are not always ready to share their knowledge without a carrot. IT tools are, of course, of utmost importance and the whole architecture of information technology should be designed with knowledge management in mind.

As far as individuals and teams are concerned, the most important things are the ability and willingness to learn and change, and to share, receive and apply knowledge. Often it is not so much about the ability as willingness. Are we really ready to share knowledge or do we believe that 'knowledge is power' and that it is not wise to give it all up. Or are we comfortable analysing and exploiting ideas and tools developed by others. The so-called NIH syndrome (Not Invented Here) is strong in many organisations.

We should not underestimate the significance of organisational culture in knowledge management. The values, feedback culture, communication habits and management styles of the organisation either help or hinder knowledge management. Eighty percent of knowledge management is change management and human resource management. The remaining twenty percent is information technology. That is why the cultural issues are so important.

Different people understand and define knowledge management in different ways, not least because we can look at it from many different viewpoints. In a way, it combines human resource management, technology management, culture and practices. Its approach is cross functional. Knowledge management supports or is supported by everything else

So far most knowledge management projects have been very much IT-oriented, which goes some of the way to explaining why they so often don't work. I believe that in the future other functions like human resources, quality and corporate planning will be more active. In fact, the need for support from so many different units of the business makes a strong case for introducing some sort of organisational structure all of its own. But in modern IT companies knowledge management is far too important to be owned by any single function. Instead, each and every employee should bear some responsibility for knowledge management. In future, every employee is going to be a knowledge manager.

What is knowledge?

What are we actually talking about when we talk about knowledge? To start with, it is not information or data, although these three things are often confused. Data is raw material that generates information. It is numbers, text, pictures or a combination of these three, and it does not contain relations or meanings. Information is data that has been changed into something with meaning. It contains some form of message and conveys something. Information is clearly sent by one person to another. The receiver determines whether it is simply a piece of data or a piece of information, an act that in itself can transform it into knowledge. Davenport and Prusak have identified the sort of events or processes that transform raw data into information, adding meaning and significance. They say that:

- when connected to an entity, we see it as a part of a more extensive entity;
- when analysed, we understand the meaning of it;
- when amended, the mistakes in the data have been corrected; and
- when compressed, raw data is presented in a clearer form.

What is knowledge then? The concept of knowledge is more extensive, more complex and more profound than information and data. The theory of knowledge (epistemology) has been studied for centuries and appears to be no closer to an agreed solution. We are dealing with some fairly fundamen-

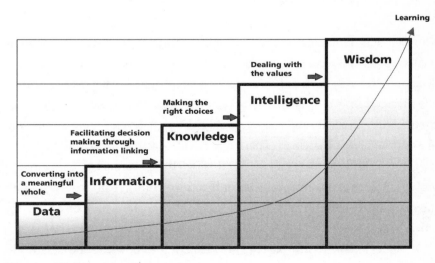

Fig. 4.4 The hierarchy of knowledge

tal questions here. But at least our task isn't to present an unchallengeable definition. We just need to describe it from a practical perspective in order to be able to understand how it can be managed and controlled.

Davenport and Prusak have come up with this definition of knowledge: it is a mixture of organised experiences, values, information and insights offering a framework to evaluate new experiences and information. Knowledge is generated and applied in the mind of the one who knows. In an organisation knowledge is often tied to documents, routines, processes, ways of working and norms.

It is important to understand that everyone is a store of knowledge. It is generated and handled in people's brains. It is both a store and a process. It is not just static but dynamic.

Davenport and Prusak argue that **information turns into knowledge**:

- By making comparisons: how does information of this situation differ from earlier corresponding situations?
- By making conclusions: what effects does information have on our decisions and actions?
- By explaining contexts: how is this information connected with other knowledge?
- By discussion: what do other people think about it?

Knowledge is generated by thought and through experiences. It is closely related to action because it can be evaluated on the basis of the decisions or actions it leads to. It is fair to say that better knowledge leads to more effective action. Knowledge is generated through experiences. A meeting, participating in a training course, reading a book, a development discussion or any other event is such an experience. According to some studies, managers get two thirds of their knowledge through direct contacts: during meetings and telephone conversations. Only a third comes from reading documents. That is why social skills are such an important part of acquiring knowledge.

Values and beliefs are part of knowledge or the knowledge process. Individual attitudes define how a person sees things and what he/she receives. That is why we need to be aware of our own values and beliefs. How we approach problems and try to solve them depends on our core values and beliefs.

So what is intelligence then? It is the right knowledge at the right time that we can use to make the right solutions, choices and decisions. Intelligence is more than knowledge. Today we talk a lot about emotional intelligence and think that it can often go a long way to explain individual success. Earlier, we described the same thing as social talent. That illustrates why knowledge in itself is not enough. We need to be able to use it. And that is where social and interpersonal skills are important. Sometimes the application of knowledge and transmitting it further can be more important than knowledge itself.

Cognitive intelligence and emotional intelligence are the key components of intelligence but they are still not enough. We need a third component – intuitive intelligence. Jagdish Parikh argues that these three components give birth to creative intelligence, a combination of cognitive, emotional and intuitive intelligence. And we need this kind of creative intelligence at this time of huge complexity and uncertainty. It is quite possible to increase our level of creative intelligence by increasing the level of consciousness. We get there by looking at the world three dimensionally.

And wisdom? Wisdom is something that is deeply internalised, the product of knowledge that we have already applied in some form. It draws together values, morals and personal experiences. Michel de Montaigne says, 'We can be clever using other people's knowledge, but we cannot be wise using other people's wisdom.' Wisdom is a result of a long personal learning process. The huge amount of knowledge that we face today just serves to emphasise the significance of values. We must be able to manage knowledge by analysing and selecting. We should be able to see the wood for the trees. Our values and the level of consciousness we use for looking at the world are paramount. Two and a half thousand years ago, Aeschylus, one of the great classical Greek dramatists, said, 'He who knows useful things, not many things, is wise.'

From the practical point of view it is broadly sufficient to concentrate on data, information and knowledge. That is challenging enough anyway. It is not always easy to differentiate between these three, but it's vital for the knowledge management process. The individual needs to go further by emphasing intelligence and wisdom as forces that steer our action. In a way, the hierarchy of knowledge represents our life-long learning journey.

So can we actually manage or control knowledge? The answer is at least partly positive. It is not as easy and simple as we might imagine. There is an intrinsic paradox. The more you try to manage, control or capture knowledge, the greater the likelihood that it changes back into information or data. And similarly, where there is too much knowledge and we cannot control or understand it, so it is degraded into information that is no longer of any real benefit to us. This is one of the frustrations of the modern knowledge society: there is so much information around but very little actual knowledge and understanding. 'Where is the wisdom we have lost in knowledge? Where is the knowledge we have lost in information?' asked the poet T. S. Eliot. Our information society is suffocating under a huge flood of information, which increasingly afflicts people with a sort of 'info cramp.'

Tacit and explicit knowledge

Knowledge is multi-dimensional. Nonaka and Takeuchi divide it into tacit and explicit. Tacit knowledge is undocumented and, accordingly, is hard to transfer to anyone else. The skills required for swimming and cycling, for example, involve tacit knowledge. We know how to do it, but it is not very easy to tell others what we do. Explicit knowledge, on the other hand, is objective and formal by nature and can be transferred to others within the organisation. We do not always realise how big a difference there is between the knowledge documented on paper or stored electronically and the knowledge embodied in our experiences, thoughts and feelings. This tacit knowledge store is, however, generally much bigger than we think. Interaction between these two kinds of knowledge creates new knowledge. Figure 4.5 illustrates the four paths to the new knowledge.

The processes describing the creation of knowledge are socialisation, externalisation, combination and internalisation. **Socialisation** is exchange of knowledge between individuals. Knowledge is transferred and created en route from one stage of tacit knowledge to the next before it becomes explicit. It is best exemplified by the traditional master–apprentice model

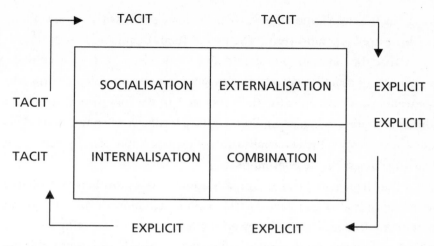

Fig. 4.5 Creation of new knowledge (Source: Nonaka and Takeuchi)

where you learn from verbal instructions, by looking and by imitating. Socialisation transfers not only knowledge and skills, but also ways of working, norms and values.

Externalisation is the transformation of tacit knowledge into explicit knowledge. Tacit becomes explicit by, for example, giving a conceptual definition. Knowledge is made visible by describing it as concretely as possible. Externalisation is valuable for an organisation, because it enables more effective sharing of knowledge.

Combination is the route from one stage of explicit knowledge to the next. Different concepts, for example, are combined to make larger entities. Combination also involves the reprocessing of knowledge.

Internalisation is the process during which explicit knowledge turns into tacit knowledge. When we internalise knowledge we are in a sense redefining it our own way. We are absorbing it to the extent that it actually begins to affect the way we think. The process of internalisation is part of renewing the individual and ultimately supports the renewal of the whole organisation.

Let's take as an example the process of a company first appreciating the value of feedback and embedding it into the way it works. An experienced manager has learnt from experience that he gets better results by giving a lot of feedback, both positive and negative. He coaches a younger colleague by telling him he should always give immediate praise when a subordinate performs well (**socialisation**). The two of them then generalise from this experience that all managers should give more feedback. They even make a formal proposal that their company will pay more attention to immediate feedback. They crystallise their thoughts in the following instruction: always give praise when possible and critical feedback when necessary. This exercise represents the **externalisation** of explicit knowledge by defining it in a form that is easy to communicate.

The management of the organisation in question here got excited about this initiative and started to think about it in more detail. They found that giving feedback is a very powerful management tool. Giving feedback is part of an open communicative culture where people are comfortable expressing themselves. In fact, they decided that this was so important that they agreed to hire a special consultant to coach all their managers about it. The training course was called 'The significance of giving feedback and feedback culture for the success of our organisation' (**combination**). The training course was a success and over the next 12 months the management of the company found the feedback culture of the organisation improved significantly. Feedback was given enthusiastically and people started to talk about things, both success and failure, openly. Feedback training was **internalised** and it had also even started to steer action on an unconscious level.

Nonaka and Takeuchi have described the creation of new knowledge in an organisation as a spiral. In addition to the four processes discussed above, the spiral illustrates the levels of the individual, the group, the organisation and the other organisations. They argue that the process of creating knowledge proceeds in a spiral through each of these processes. All the phases are important: socialisation prepares externalisation, externalisation is a condition for combination, and good combination helps to internalise things. Figure 4.6 illustrates this theory. It is not immediately accessible but it rewards perseverance because it describes something very powerful.

It goes without saying that organisational learning is more effective if there are no limits to staff's potential for innovation. There must be plenty of sources of knowledge running throughout the company. Nonaka and

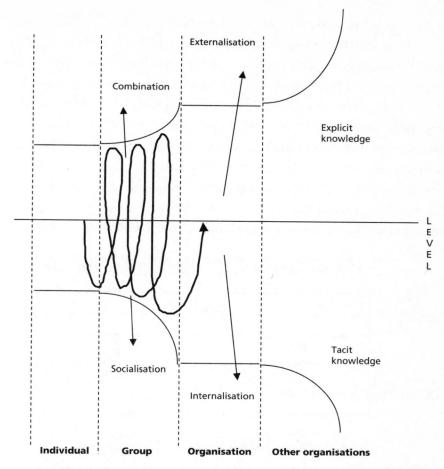

Fig. 4.6 The spiral of creating knowledge in an organisation (According to Nonaka and Takeuchi)

Takeuchi say over-supply is not a disadvantage because the organisation's sense of purpose will ultimately forge that into something productive.

The flow of knowledge in an organisation

Understanding the different properties of data, information and knowledge is important to laying the groundwork for implementing effective policy. So is the idea of tacit and explicit knowledge. Sharing knowledge is all about transforming one into the other, which ultimately enables the organisation to accumulate as much knowledge as possible.

Building this explicit knowledge is the organisation's ultimate goal. Once it is in that form, and fused throughout the company's operations, it can't walk out in the way an employee can disappear. This sort of knowledge still only represents a fairly small share of the organisation's data bank. The figure is probably hovering somewhere between 10–20 percent. But the share could easily be doubled by effective knowledge management. And that in turn would have the effect of improving and safeguarding the competitiveness of the organisation for the future. Figure 4.7 shows how information gets transformed into the organisation's explicit knowledge.

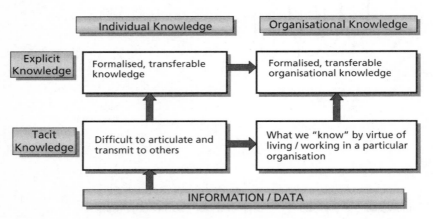

Fig. 4.7   The areas of knowledge and creation of knowledge in an organisation

We need to better understand the significance of tacit knowledge in an organisation. Western countries have traditionally only really valued explicit, measurable knowledge. But in Japan and other countries of the East they have appreciated the importance of tacit knowledge and they can use it better. They have understood that there is a lot of knowledge that we are not necessarily always aware of either on an individual or an organisational level.

Even though we understand the importance of tacit knowledge, we should learn how to share it more effectively. We should identify the areas of knowledge that can only be transferred by common experience and facilitate that process. In some respects, sharing tacit knowledge is returning to the old master–apprentice model. The present interest in mentoring is most probably based on this type of need.

Knowledge management in practice

Consider whether some of these ideas about knowledge management could be implemented in your own organisation. Is the environment fertile for these sort of things? Is knowledge so important that it should be separately managed? What kind of benefits would the implementation of knowledge management bring to the organisation? Would it, for example, help cut costs, increase income, or improve operations? How could we implement the knowledge management project in practice?

From strategy to business benefits through knowledge management

Figure 4.8 shows how to get from strategy to actually benefiting business from effective knowledge management. It involves establishing the role of knowledge in all the different elements of the business.

Fig. 4.8   From strategy to business benefits through knowledge management

The starting point for knowledge management is the analysis of the present situation. What sort of knowledge, for example, is required by the organisation's performance and competence management process? Is there enough knowledge, is new knowledge generated efficiently enough, is enough knowledge captured from outside the business, does the company know how to store its knowledge, is knowledge shared enough, how is it applied, and can we exploit or reuse the knowledge that already exists in the organisation? You should go through all these questions. If you are satisfied with the answers, you probably don't need to spend too much time on knowledge management. But if you are not satisfied, you need to think about whether the processes in your organisation are adequate. Do you continuously try to improve the processes and do you use a 'best practices' approach? Then you need to think about how the organisational structure supports knowledge management. Is any attention paid to teamwork, virtual teams and information flow in teams? Are people aware of how important knowledge management is and do they share their knowledge? How does the organisational culture support knowledge management? Is the culture open enough and built on confidence? Do people appreciate how empowering it can be to share knowledge? And last, but not least, comes technology. Have the existing systems been designed with knowledge management in mind? And how can IT be exploited more effectively?

We can use Fig. 4.8 as a sort of checklist of the present situation. Before any knowledge management project is started, we need to be able to define future benefits. That's the only way to convince ourselves of the usefulness of the project. And this model may also help to sell a knowledge management project to the management. They are generally only really interested in final results.

First steps in implementation

The model 'From Strategy to Business Benefits' should be considered in the preliminary phase. It provides a good basis for any upcoming decisions. We need to determine whether we actually need a knowledge management project and we must know where to invest first. If we go on, it is good to go through the first steps of knowledge management presented in Fig. 4.9. The model describes some of the most important phases of the situation when the knowledge management project is eventually implemented.

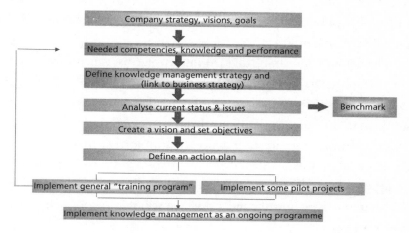

Fig. 4.9   First steps in the implementation of knowledge management

The first phase starts by analysing the strategy, vision and objectives of the organisation. What is our target and what kind of performance is needed to achieve this goal? What kind of competence do we need and, in particular, what knowledge do we need?

Think about the following questions:

- What is the importance of knowledge for business?
- What is critical knowledge?
- How is knowledge managed and controlled?
- How do we define the subprocesses of knowledge management (the creation, capturing, storing, sharing and application of knowledge)?

Here we formulate the framework and decide what we mean when we talk about knowledge management. We must also establish how it is linked to other processes, like performance and competence management.

The resulting framework determines the next stages. It is easier if you have a reference point, like another comparable business that has undergone a similar process, but you should already have a pretty clear set of objectives of your own. Set priorities and targets and develop an action plan. Very often, companies think of this process as being a one-off event, but it is probably most effective if at this stage you ingrain the idea that you are developing a separate and permanent function into the business. It will eventually become routine.

The action plan can be divided into two areas: general training and some pilot projects. The former means training key people and enhancing their awareness of the importance of knowledge management. We introduce them to the framework of knowledge management and give concrete examples of what it means in practice. It is important that they have the right attitude towards the exercise so that they take a positive approach to sharing knowledge. Planning and development discussions should also include an item asking how the individual contributes to knowledge sharing in the company.

The other part of the action plan is to start some pilot projects. It is often a good way to start by testing one's own ideas in concrete small-scale projects. These projects help us to analyse our thoughts and the results can be presented as encouraging examples. After these first experiments it is worth a final reappraisal of the detail of the strategy and content of the knowledge management project before implementing it as a long-term project.

People, culture and technology are the critical factors for the success of knowledge management projects. Firstly, people will have to change their attitudes towards knowledge management and understand that the active sharing of knowledge is a part of everybody's job description. Everyone must also understand his or her role as a receiver of knowledge, that he or she will have to change from a passive 'receiver' to an active 'searcher'. The likelihood in a big company is that so many people benefit from shared knowledge that the sender can not pick them individually. That means it is important that the sender can 'package' the piece of knowledge into a form that is easy to receive.

Secondly, organisational culture is very important. It needs to be open and support direct and honest communication. The organisation must have enough confidence capital. This means that everyone trusts that you promote your own and your organisation's success by sharing knowledge. And it is important that the organisation has a commonly shared concrete vision and strategy.

Thirdly, knowledge management needs the support of the latest IT technology. The IT architecture of the organisation must be planned so that data moves fluently in different applications.

In practice, knowledge management can be very different things. We shall go through three examples – an Intranet application of a human resource management system (HR Notes), the evaluation of the efficiency of distributing knowledge, and the creation and use of management training material (a Black Book).

An Intranet application of a human resource management system

The HR Notes application was first used at Nokia in 1997. The application aims to maintain and efficiently share knowledge about personnel data. It includes process descriptions, working instructions, tools, forms, and policies. It can also be used to discuss specific topics.

The application is in use globally. It has three target groups. Firstly, the whole staff can see the latest and most updated version of the different procedures and policies. This kind of global application makes knowledge distribution efficient and easy, and it means that its audience knows where to look for more knowledge. The second target group is the human resource professionals. They can use it to distribute information that is meant only for them, for example, confidential information about salary. The third target group is the different HR project groups. They can set up project pages in the system that allows access only to the members of a given group. This kind of database application in the organisation's internal network is a typical knowledge management tool. It makes knowledge distribution much more effective and it doesn't take long before you wonder how you ever did without it. The biggest problem is updating the data. It is easy to accumulate too much data and convolute its efficiency. So it is important to maintain and edit the data so that it is as 'easy' to read as possible. It probably requires a person whose full-time job is to manage the content.

The efficiency of knowledge distribution

Have you ever thought how efficiently the process of knowledge distribution is implemented in your organisation? What percentage score would you give your own unit? Matti Verkasalo has studied the efficiency of knowledge distribution at Nokia and written his doctoral thesis on the subject. He says the efficiency index of knowledge distribution is normally just 20–30 percent. But the index is easy to double if you use efficient data systems for knowledge distribution.

Verkasalo's thesis focuses on identifying the bottle-necks in the distribution of specialist knowledge and on the development of knowledge distribution systems. The study defines the different phases of the knowledge exploitation process and develops a method to measure the efficiency of the optional knowledge distribution techniques.

There are different phases of the knowledge exploitation process: capture, documentation, transfer, reception, understanding and decision-making. The efficiency index method measures the efficiency of these, focusing on three variables: the delay in knowledge distribution, the scope of knowledge distribution and the amount of work needed in the different phases of knowledge distribution. The study found that it was possible to increase the index from 20–30 percent to between 50 and 80 percent. More effective exploitation of knowledge offers a real competitive advantage, especially to companies operating in quickly changing markets.

From tacit to explicit knowledge in management work

The third example is related to the transformation of tacit knowledge into explicit knowledge in the development process of managers. In our own unit we often asked ourselves how we could improve the quality of management practice in a product development environment. Managers were offered a lot of training opportunities but we often felt that this learning was not very effectively implemented. We also knew we had plenty of experienced, good managers who were highly skilled in many different areas of management. So we asked ourselves how we could transfer this 'know-how' from these experienced managers to the younger ones.

This is when we came up with the idea of the so-called Black Book. We wanted to gather all this tacit knowledge into a small booklet. So we established a small working group and invited a few experienced department managers to become members. The target of this working group was to gather and crystallise the basics of good management practice. We chose seven areas of management: visions, products, processes, projects, management of teams, management of individuals, and self-management. Our purpose was to find the seven most important themes for each area. It meant the booklet would contain 50–60 pages (7 x 7). The majority of the content was supposed to be pictures, graphs, aphorisms, and worksheets. Then we tried to re-edit all knowledge so that it would be easy to use.

When the booklet was finished it was well received. It can be used in many ways. It helps each individual to consider the key management issues and helps older managers coach their younger colleagues in management practice. It has been used as material in a one-day training course for all managers in product development and has been used as material for mentor groups.

The Black Book is a good example of knowledge management. It processes knowledge through Nonaka's phases of socialisation, externalisation, combination and internalisation. In the first phase we noticed that there was a lot of tacit knowledge in an organisation that should be transformed into explicit knowledge. We formed a working group where we gathered this tacit knowledge and edited it into explicit knowledge we could share with the whole managerial staff. Then we arranged some training sessions and put together the material we had produced. The package described the basic elements of successful management. The idea is that people will repeat things after the training course and continue discussions with superiors and colleagues. Then they will adopt what they have learnt and see the results in practice. The Black Book is also a good example of how knowledge can be managed and processed without the help of complex information technology.

Intellectual capital and its measurement

Knowledge has become an important competitive advantage and the organisation's success depends upon the competence of its employees. That's why we have started to talk about intellectual capital alongside traditional financial capital. The market value of the company depends on a combination of these factors. Intellectual capital can, to an extent, be defined as the difference between the company's market value and its book value. In many IT companies this difference is huge. But, that difference does not in practice depend solely on the company's intellectual capital. The company's market value can vary a lot for reasons unrelated to intellectual capital. A lot of speculation and assumption about the company's future prospects are factored into the market value. In fact, a third factor influencing the market value is the company's future expectations. We call it 'expectation' capital. Figure 4.10 shows the capital structure of the organisation.

Intellectual capital is the sum of structural and human capital. The competence of the employees, their knowledge, skills, attitudes, experiences and contacts are human capital. The company can't own human capital but it generally does own structural capital, things like databases, registers, manuals, and brands. In a sense, structural capital is what is left behind when the employees leave the workplace.

Structural capital is divided into customer capital and organisational capital. Organisational capital is then further subdivided into innovation capital, process capital, culture capital and core competence capital. Organisational culture is not normally classified as a kind of capital, but I think it has a considerable impact on the success of the company and, through that, on the market value. Core competence, in my opinion, is also a form of organisational capital. Each organisation has some special competence upon which to build its operations. The building of such organisational core competence normally takes a long time and it is not easy for competitors to copy it.

Knowledge management means trying to manage and control the intellectual capital of the company. To do it successfully means looking after both the human capital and the structures that facilitate that being trans-

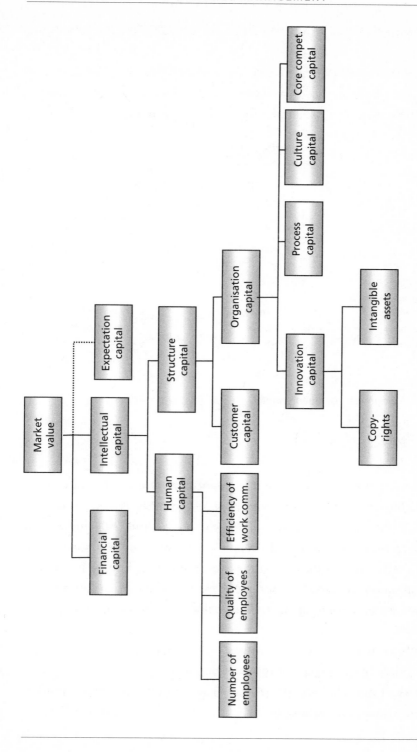

Fig. 4.10 Capital structure of the organisation

formed into the organisational competence that ultimately generates the revenue.

Human capital is divided into three components: the number of employees, the quality of those employees and the efficiency of the entire work community. Figure 4.11 illustrates these areas by examples.

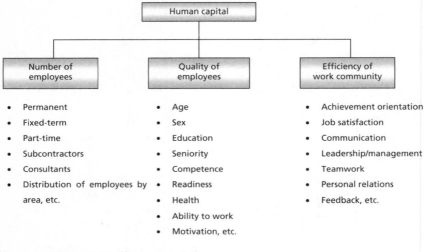

Fig. 4.11   Components of human capital

Employee account

As human capital has become such an important success factor for companies, we have started to think about how best to measure and evaluate it. An 'employee account' is one way of doing it. It is basically a document that attempts to make a sort of public report of the company's human capital. Some of it is based on the company's conventional accounting but it does not really conform to any laws or regulations. Guy Ahonen suggests a working employee account be characterised by the following principles:

- It is the company's official account of their human resources and the development of these resources.
- It gives a realistic picture of different factors connected to the long-term performance of the employees.

- It gives information that helps the external financial stakeholders of the company to form a picture of the company's sustainable result development.
- It steers the company's strategic and operative management to use and develop the human resources of the company correctly.
- Its data have been confirmed by parties with sufficient authority.
- It is narrow and general but also sufficiently detailed to work as a tool for company assessment.
- Its concepts have been defined so that its data is comparable with the corresponding data of other companies.

The employee account is divided into three parts (see Fig. 4.12). Employee reports are drafted in almost all companies, but an employee income statement and balance sheet is probably very rare. Different kinds of 'employee accounts' are made in many companies, but this information is generally considered so confidential that it is not published outside the company. The comparability of this sort of information is also problematic: it is industry-specific and this kind of data can be difficult to compare even within the same industry. It is also not necessarily always a very meaningful exercise try to to attach a monetary value to this sort of thing. Apart from anything, that raises the risk that the tax authorities will try to grab their share.

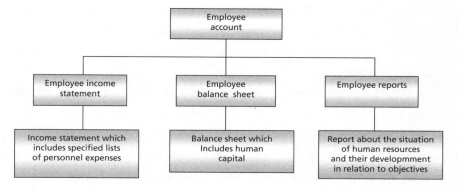

Fig. 4.12 Employee account

There are, of course, many reasons why we can justify the necessity of an official employee account. If human capital is the company's most important source of income and accounts for the majority of the market value, it is important for the company to know precisely what it is so that it can better manage it. This kind of information is also valued in the marketplace. Secondly, it is a good way of effectively allocating human resources throughout the organisation. They enable the company to work out more exactly how much they should apportion to any given operation, and to better balance workloads. Employee accounts are still in a developmental phase and it isn't altogether clear how they will evolve. But they can be a useful tool for human resource departments and top level management.

Summary and conclusions

Knowledge and knowledge management was one of the hottest fads of the late 1990s in the world of human resources. But it remains unclear exactly what it is and what value it offers. There is still a lot of work to be done if we are to transform it from a passing fad into something genuinely practical and effective.

For an individual, knowledge is analysed experiences, insights, values and information aggregated to form the framework with which new experiences and information are further evaluated. Knowledge is always highly subjective but it can be shared by acquiring common frameworks. And that's where knowledge management comes in because knowledge is both a store and a process. It has its own hierarchy: data, information, knowledge, intelligence and wisdom.

Knowledge management is a process that creates, captures, stores, shares and applies knowledge. The objective is to improve the quality of decision-making. Knowledge management is about turning individual knowledge into organisational knowledge and tacit knowledge into explicit knowledge. The objective is to turn as much knowledge as possible into explicit organisational knowledge. Knowledge is refined through socialisation, externalisation, combination and internalisation. The ultimate aim is the free flow of knowledge in the organisation.

We can start the analysis of knowledge management in the organisation by answering the following questions:

- What is the significance of knowledge in business?
- What kind of knowledge is critical for us?
- How do we manage and control knowledge?
- How do we define the subprocesses of knowledge management?
- What are the biggest problems in knowledge management?
- What can we concretely do to improve knowledge management?

The company capital can be divided into the following areas:

- Financial capital
- Customer-bound capital
- Organisation-bound capital
- Employee-bound capital
- Industry/company expectation-bound capital

Employee-bound capital forms a crucial part of the company's total capital. In the future companies should be able to measure this capital better and report on the results in public, perhaps in the form of an employee account.

Chapter 5
An Intelligent Organisation

No limits to the future
There are no limits to the human imagination.
There are no limits to our capacity for change.
There are no limits to our capability to improve.
There are no limits to our willingness to achieve.
There are no limits to our dedication to serve.
There are no limits except those we set ourselves.
There are no limits.

Nokia's Annual Report 1999

Towards an intelligent organisation

We are all familiar with the concept of a learning organisation. We have been talking about it for almost twenty years. But the evolution of the learning organisation is still half-finished and the concept remains somewhat problematic. It is not altogether clear, for example, that there are any organisations that don't learn. So it is more about the companies that develop the structures and culture that enable them to learn quickly.

As well as learning, we increasingly talk about the end results of learning, such as competence. Competence is an important resource in the intelligent organisation. Hannus, Lindroos and Seppänen (1999) call this present era 'the age of competence'. It describes a period during which competence has become a critical resource and technology gives us the tools to build totally new kinds of structures and mechanisms for adding value. Hamel (2000) has gone even further by naming our era 'the age of revolution,' where it is not simply knowledge but insight into opportunities for discontinuous innovation which produces new wealth.

Learning is one of the crucial factors in the ideal organisation of the future, but by no means the only one. The successful organisations of the future will need to be efficient, extracting top performance from all their units. And that will require greater collective intelligence, bred from knowledge, competence and understanding. It is this kind of intelligence that will really make the difference.

Thus the ideal organisation of the future can be described as **an intelligent organisation**, which means being capable of continuous renewal, of anticipating changes and of learning fast. A truly intelligent organisation will be adaptive to the ferocious pace of change. And rather than being mechanical, it will look more like a living organism that can steer its own operations.

The intelligent organisation will also handle knowledge in a versatile way because knowledge is ever-changing. It has no absolute value per se so the objective is to apply and develop it according to the needs of circumstance. That means understanding knowledge before it can be effectively applied. So one of the keys to the effective application of knowledge is understanding. Because if the company does not fully understand the implications of its knowledge then it will not be able to extract maximum value.

Today's hectic organisations do not always pay enough attention to the significance of understanding, which means they often fail to get the most out of applying their knowledge to a given situation. Understanding takes time, time for reflection. An intelligent organisation reserves enough time for reflection on an individual, a team and an organisational level. Figure 5.1 shows the staircase of knowledge in an intelligent organisation.

An intelligent organisation is always trying to reach the top step, where it can develop its knowledge base. This is how it preserves its ability to see things from a fresh viewpoint. Development demands experimentation, innovation, and improvisation. We must be able to look at things with a new pair of eyes, to challenge the rigidities of our thought processes. Once we had a Thai cave monk called Ajahn Sumano Bhikkhu training us at Nokia. The subject was the development of our own internal resources and creativ-

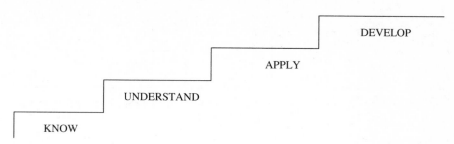

Fig. 5.1 Staircase of knowledge in an intelligent organisation

ity. His viewpoint was different from ours. That was exactly why we had such a productive occasion with ground-breaking dialogue, not just in verbal form, but on a higher level too. For renewal we need different kinds of mirrors to assess our own ways of thinking.

Peter Drucker has likened an intelligent organisation to a jazz band. The predominant organisational model nowadays is more like a symphony orchestra, where the leader behaves like the conductor. Each member of the orchestra has his or her carefully defined role agreed upon in advance. But the intelligent organisation of the future should be more like a jazz band, composing its music as it goes along. It improvises, renews itself and changes continuously. It has come to a common agreement on the target, but the means to achieve that target can continuously change.

The features of an intelligent organisation

An intelligent organisation has the ability to renew itself continuously, foresee changes and learn fast. How can an organisation develop to be that way? What kind of factors is such an organisation built upon? Figure 5.2 shows some of the features of an intelligent organisation.

An organisation must have a clear vision and strategy. We need more visionary management in organisations. Their ideas must give energy to the whole organisation because they are ultimately what describe the real purpose of the organisation. Vision must be shared and it must concretely be divided into sub-visions. Furthermore, communication and understanding must play a key role. A vision that you don't understand cannot steer your action.

13 LEADERSHIP BY TEACHING - participating - self management	14 ABILITY TO CHANGE IS HIGH	1 CLEAR VISION AND STRATEGY - shared - communicated	2 ORGANISATION STRUCTURE SUPPORTING RENEWAL - virtual, team,process	3 CULTURE AND VALUES - sustainable development - customer satisfaction - respect for the individual
12 USING TECHNOLOGY AS ENABLER		**AN INTELLIGENT ORGANISATION** - ability to foresee changes, learn fast and renew itself continuously		4 CONTINUOUS IMPROVEMENT IDEOLOGY IN PLACE
11 FEEDBACK SYSTEMS				5 HUMAN RESOURCE MANAGEMENT IS APPRECIATED
10 TEAM MANAGEMENT	9 KNOWLEDGE MANAGEMENT	8 COMPETENCE MANAGEMENT	7 PERFORMANCE MANAGEMENT	6 CLEAR PROCESSES - core and support processes

Fig. 5.2   The features of an intelligent organisation

The structure of an intelligent organisation supports renewal. There should be no extra barriers. It is a modern, virtual team and process organisation. It has a common vision and objective, but everything else is changing continuously. This kind of organisation consists of competence centres supplying a product or service to those who need it. Core competencies are kept inside the organisation but elsewhere the boundaries are difficult to define. Figure 5.3 shows the structure of an intelligent organisation of the future where all units work in teams in different kinds of competence centres inside the organisation (square) or outside it.

This kind of organisation is constantly evolving. Tomorrow it will be different from how it is today. New competence centres are connected to it while others are removed. Some parts of the organisation are intentionally temporary. There are also functional and hierachical features. It has simultaneously connected together all the different organisational models that it needs for any given situation. Most importantly, the organisation is not an end in itself, but a way of working to achieve an objective.

An intelligent organisation is managed with a clear and distinct set of values in mind. They steer the way it manages its operations and are integral to the culture that it tries to create. It understands its own special values as well as universal values such as respect for the individual, continuous learning and sustainable development. In the future, employees will choose

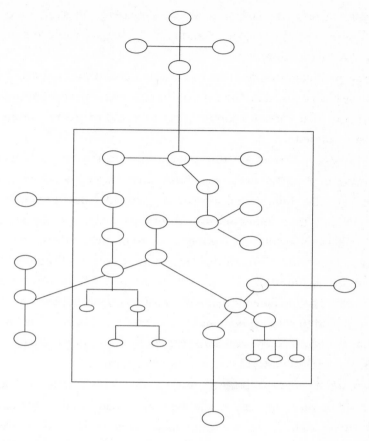

Fig. 5.3   The structure of an intelligent organisation

their employer more and more on the basis of the values the organisation represents.

   This concept of continuous improvement is the basis of all operations. If you don't want to be better, you are no longer any good, said Abraham Lincoln. Quality management is built into all processes and ways of working. And as we know, quality ultimately depends upon the attitude of each individual because it is the result of everybody doing their best.

   An intelligent organisation will have invested heavily in performance management, which is embedded into other processes at different levels of the organisation. Competence management and knowledge management are crucial parts of its performance management. A renewed performance management process guarantees that the targets set are achieved, competence is systematically developed, and knowledge is available to everybody within the organisation.

An intelligent organisation has clearly defined processes. The processes have been defined on the basis of the customers' needs. The organisations define their core and support processes and these are continuously being streamlined.

Heavy investments are also made in human resource management. Employees are the company's most important resource and so a lot of significance is attached to human resource management. Good human resource management is the number one priority of top management. Special attention is paid to the employees' competence and motivation. Employee satisfaction is monitored through regular employee surveys. People are at the heart of the organisation.

Because an intelligent organisation works mainly in teams, a lot of attention is paid to management and the organising of teams. The organisation has defined its own model for teamwork, constantly evaluates how it works, and has built reward systems with this in mind.

An intelligent organisation gathers feedback systematically. The feedback systems work throughout the organisation and feedback is seen as a condition for all learning, development and change. The 360-degree feedback surveys, as well as balanced scorecard approaches, are an everyday routine of the organisation. The feedback culture should also support open dialogue, which means open discussion that promotes the best ideas.

Information technology is efficiently exploited. There is a lot of thought given to how it enables the development of new ways of working. And it has not only an implementing role, but increasingly has an enabling one. The new technology brings with it totally new mechanisms for value creation. Company operations are managed by comprehensive systems (Enterprise Resource Planning) that combine all the functions of the organisation. And it is supported by all the different types of intranet and working group system technologies.

Management is seen as a service function, with the task of organising success. It needs to be applied from every different angle. Team management, participating management, coaching and self leadership are perspectives in which an intelligent organisation is ready to invest. It is always looking for new dimensions in management.

Ultimately the most important feature of an intelligent organisation is its readiness for change and renewal, even when there is no immediate change ahead. The organisation invests in this feature even when operations are successful, perhaps even more so. We must remember the saying: There is nothing to save a successful organisation. We must regard change as a natural condition. Every employee is ready for a fresh approach and does not just aspire to what has always been done.

Management in an intelligent organisation

In today's global and turbulent world, management has become more challenging. Not least because it has been besieged by different fads that only give a one-sided or mono-dimensional insight into management challenges. We need to be able to examine things comprehensively but we also need to be able to simplify and focus on the key issues. This is a big challenge for today's managers; how to combine comprehensiveness and simplification. How do you manage in a comprehensively simplified way?

Management in a global village demands an ability to see the business from a range of viewpoints:

- individual;
- team, department, unit;
- organisation/company;
- industry;
- country;
- continent; and
- globe.

These relationships also have to be explored from different perspectives:

- economic;
- technological;
- political;
- social;
- ecological; and
- spiritual viewpoint.

Figure 5.4 drafts the different dimensions of management in the global world.

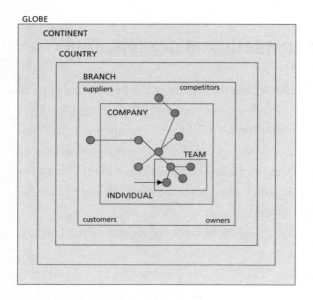

Fig. 5.4 Management in a global world

Ultimately, my own vision of management is just as limited as all the others. I put the emphasis on the key role that people play.

During the next few years we need to invest especially in visionary management, strategic management, performance management and self leadership. These helps us in the following way:

- visionary management gives a purpose to our action and answers the question **why**;
- strategic management gives a direction to our action and answers the question **what**;
- performance management steers our daily actions and answers the question **how**; and
- self leadership enables action on an individual level and answers the question '**with what energy?**'

Visionary management

Each organisation needs a time-bound vision steering its operations. The vision must be simple and clear. It must be effective and strong. There are feelings, hopes and dreams attached to this vision. The vision presented by Kennedy about Americans being the first people to land on the moon by the year 1970 is a perfect example of this kind of vision.

The culmination of Nokia's vision was four themes formulated by Ollila (focus, information technology, global, added value) that steered Nokia's operations effectively in the 90s. Now Nokia's vision is the building of a mobile information society. What could be more inspiring? Here is an example of how it has been articulated in a letter from Jorma Ollila and Pekka Ala-Pietilä in Nokia's Annual Report 1999. 'We are at the beginning of something very significant. Not just for our company. Not just for our industry. But for everyone. And for all aspects of our lives. We are using the twin drivers of the Internet and mobility to break through the limits of time and place. These are very powerful forces. And at this stage no one can say precisely where they will lead us to. But we are sure that it will be a very special time.'

Vision management demands intuition and courage. We need to be prepared for all possible future directions. We must be able to look far enough ahead into the future and open a new track. That is not always an easy task and it is why visionaries or charismatic leaders are always in short supply.

Creating visions is a process of building significance and understanding. With the help of the visions we generate energy inside the organisations, which in turn generates enthusiasm, feeling and inspiration. An intelligent organisation is also emotionally intelligent because people and organisations do not always function logically. An intelligent organisation demands creative intelligence formed of cognitive, emotional and intuitive intelligence. It values culture, beliefs, intuition and feelings, all the things that have historically been ignored because of their intangibility.

A vision give us a framework through which we interpret events. Every member of the organisation needs his or her own vision. It is one thing to pile bricks on top of each other day after day but something quite different to build the world's biggest cathedral.

Strategic management

We plot the route from the present to our future vision by making strategic choices. The significance of strategy cannot be over-emphasised. If you have chosen the wrong road, it doesn't matter how fast you run. Operative efficiency cannot compensate for strategic mistakes.

Strategic management requires the ability to create visions. We need to be capable of conceptual thinking and root this ability at every level of the organisation. We must use systematic thinking: see extensive relationships and understand things comprehensively. After all, everything is interrelated. Strategy gives us a focus, a tool to make choices and differentiate ourselves from the competition.

Strategic management is a continuous process. The strategy is planned, implemented, tested and developed on a continuous basis. We look at our compass all the time, not just once a year.

In an intelligent organisation all employees participate in the development of strategy. Conceptual thinking and seeing things in their entirety are important capabilities. Strategic thinking is widespread and strategies are constantly being discussed and evolved.

Performance management

A general rule of an intelligent organisation is that it simplifies, crystallises, concentrates on essentials and sees entities. That means avoiding too much fashionable thinking and new fad terms, but instead building the terminology on the basis of concepts that are already familiar to the organisation. More often than not these days the new jargon thrown at us by management consultants just confuses the picture.

So what is really essential in managing an organisation? Figure 5.5 presents a simple model. There are just three basic concepts (but if anyone wants more terms from the fad-box at the bottom of the picture, you can take your pick). Good results are achieved by good performance management, which in its expanded form should include knowledge and competence management. But good results need to be looked at imaginatively, on both an operative and a business level. They do not always show the same results, which generally signifies a failure of strategic management. And effective strategic management requires the capacity both for vision and for turning that vision into a reality. Truly great businesses create their own markets this way.

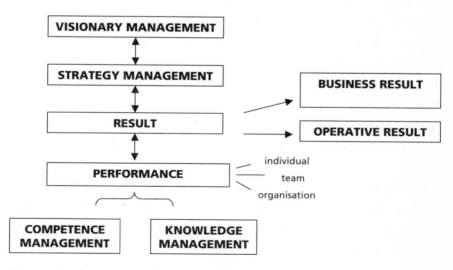

Fig. 5.5 The management of an organisation in a nutshell

Different fads

Quality management, management by objectives, value management, change management, resource management, process management, situational leadership, lean management, self-management, human resource management, strategic management, people management, activity-based management, navigating management, interactive management, management by objectives, management by teaching, management by results.

Performance management is the basic level of management and needs a lot of attention. It should be managed on an individual, a team and an organisational level and the different levels should be integrated with each other. This new framework of performance management collects and simplifies all the essential issues we have been talking about – performance, competence and knowledge management.

The processes of performance, competence and knowledge management are overlapping and any new framework should concentrate on taking care of the issues in the overlapping area. These are the really important issues. One of the key tasks of performance management is to support organisational learning and we should ensure that it goes further than a change in the environment around us. That is what allows us to control change. Figure 5.6 shows the most important factors in the new framework of the performance management process.

In an intelligent organisation the process of performance management is used to steer operations effectively on an individual, a team and an organisational level. Performance management is integrated into other management systems and incorporates competence and knowledge management.

The responsibility of performance management is divided between the individual, the team and the manager. They are all responsible for it. The model of self leadership is the main management model and employees steer their own operations both independently and in teams.

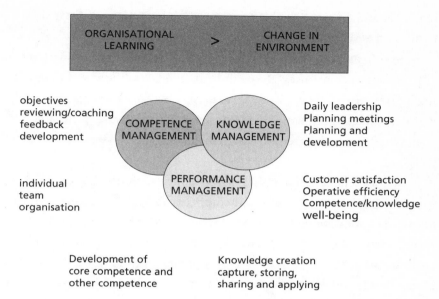

objectives
reviewing/coaching
feedback
development

Daily leadership
Planning meetings
Planning and
development

individual
team
organisation

Customer satisfaction
Operative efficiency
Competence/knowledge
well-being

Development of
core competence and
other competence

Knowledge creation
capture, storing,
sharing and applying

Fig. 5.6   The most important factors of the new performance management system

Self leadersip

There are many kinds of management but the basis of all management is self leadership. If you cannot lead yourself well, you probably cannot lead others well either.

Self leadership has been emphasised a lot during the last ten years. Organisations have become leaner; traditional power bases inside them have weakened; we are more beholden to teamwork as well as autonomy. Management training increasingly focused on self leadership during the 1990s. It is not always easy to define what kind of managers we will need in the future but we do know that they will have one feature in common: they will be good self-leaders. They will have high self-esteem and self-knowledge. They will be strong personalities. They will be flexible and fast learners who can cope in totally unexpected situations.

We are all managing directors of our own company. Our organisation is called Self Ltd. We should be able to manage this entity well. Self Ltd is divided into departments, such as the physical, mental, social and spiritual departments. We must be able to manage the operations of these departments and functions and the interaction between them.

Another way to describe self leadership is to talk about total wellness. Top performance requires people to be in good condition, and maintaining high standards demands total wellness. There are five areas that make up total wellness – professional, physical, mental, social and spiritual condition. When our wellness curve is high in all these areas, we are efficient and feel good.

Self leadership also consists of very concrete things. It means having clear objectives in work, sufficient competence, feedback about performance and continuous development. Physical condition means that I eat, exercise, sleep and rest enough. Mental condition means that I am energetic, curious, fast in making decisions and learning new things. Social condition means that I can take care of my relationship, my children, my parents, my friends, my hobbies. Spiritual condition, again, means that the purpose and values of my life are in balance – I have clear objectives and spiritual stimuli steering my life.

Good self leadership releases energy and gives new internal resources. It is a tool to fight against fatigue, over-specialisation and boredom. We all have plenty of unused resources and it is perfectly possible to unlock these internal resources. Often our own restricted views are the biggest obstacles to change, growth and development. Start the development of management from inside.

Human resource management in an intelligent organisation

Good human resource management is one of the characteristics of an intelligent organisation. It knows that success depends on competent and motivated employees. Human resource management is all about people management and line managers bear the main responsibility. The role of the human resource function is to support and steer human resource management throughout the organisation. Employees are seen as the most impor-

tant resource of the company and the strategic significance of human resource management is emphasised. The ultimate role of human resource
management is to support the organisation and its members to achieve their
objectives.

The general vision of human resource management

A general vision of human resource management is to create, maintain and
develop:

- efficient organisations so that they are competitive;
- learning organisations so that they can succeed in the future; and
- 'well-being' organisations so that employees are motivated and have the
  energy to work in the long term.

An intelligent organisation can correctly emphasise these factors and find
a suitable balance between them all. That is what success is all about in the
long term.

It is also healthy to be able to see the person and his values that under-
pins human resource management. Good human resource management is
based on respect for the individual and doesn't treat people just as a resource
or a cost factor. It should be familiar with the different aspects of the individual and support his or her comprehensive growth. It should be sensitive
to their total wellbeing and make sure that it is part of planning and development discussions.

Treating an employee as a person in their own right is all part of embedding humanist values in the organisation. But it is also about preparing
for future success. Top performance demands strong competence, commitment, profound and extensive conceptual perception and understanding.
Only someone who feels appreciated can produce the energy needed. That
is why the human factor is the success factor of the future in a top organisation.

The new roles of the human resource manager

The company management expects a great deal these days of human resource directors and managers, because the competitiveness of the organisations depends more and more on the employees. A lot of faith is put into performance, competence and knowledge management and results are expected to materialise quickly. That's why a human resource manager has many roles. He or she must be a doer, developer, innovator and visionary at the same time, to borrow some of David Ulrich's taxonomy.

The doer performs the traditional functions of human resource administration. The developer takes care of the competence and motivation of the employees. The innovator implements change and needs to be an expert in change management. A visionary looks for new directions and perspectives and is an expert in strategic and visionary management. These different roles are the staircase of human resource management. The steps described in Fig. 5.7 include the sort of tasks required of the job these days.

Human resource directors have their work cut out both now and in the future. To succeed, a human resource director has to be a trend-setter, must know how to persuade people, and be comfortable selling his or her ideas

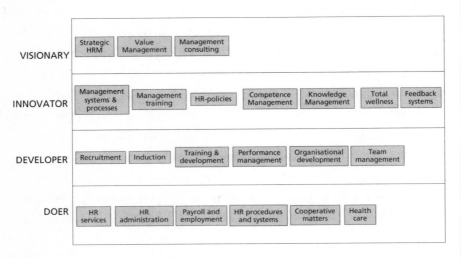

Fig. 5.7 The roles and tasks of human resource management

to other people. Matti Alahuhta has defined the human resource function as a partner bringing added value. These are the sort of expectations he described for HR directors at the 1997 HR Management Conference hosted by the Management Centre Europe:

- understands the business well;
- is up-to-date with latest trends and best practices;
- is proactive and practical;
- can listen to the organisation;
- is flexible, but goal-oriented;
- can prioritise; and
- implements things efficiently.

Figure 5.8 shows the competence profile of the Human Resource Director that came out of a planning and development discussion with my own superior a few years ago. The profile clearly shows the sort of expectations and competence required of Human Resource Directors. It is beginning to look more and more like a management consultant role. In fact, Human Resource Directors must be able to adopt this expanded role or it will be externalised and outsourced to management consulting companies that are already rapidly expanding their operations into this area at the moment.

The future focus areas of human resource management

PA Consulting Group studied Finnish human resource practice in the summer of 1999. The target group of the study was the 300 biggest Finnish companies and 50 public sector organisations. 125 forms were returned (a return rate of 36 percent). The results did a good job of describing the present challenges of human resource management. Figure 5.9 shows the ten most important focus areas. The diagram describes the key areas during the last three years and what they will be for the next three years.

The study predicted the following:

	1	2	3	4	5
1. STRATEGIC CAPABILITY - seeks involvement in strategy formulation and contributes to the development of business strategies - develops and implements coherent and integrated HR-strategies in support of business plans	1	2	3	4	5
2. BUSINESS AWARENESS - understands the activities, processes and technology of the business - identifies opportunities to contribute to creating added value and enhancing competitive advantage and intervenes as necessary	1	2	3	4	5
3. PROFESSIONAL DEVELOPMENT AND UNDERSTANDING - continually improves and extends professional knowledge and skills - ensures that the line management colleagues understand the significance of new developments and "own " any new or changed processes	1	2	3	4	5
4. INTERNAL CONSULTANCY - systematically analyses organisational and people issues to produce practical ideas for improvements - coaches line managers in identifying organisational and people issues and implementing improvements	1	2	3	4	5
5. ORGANISATIONAL EFFECTIVENESS - understands the key factors which contribute organisational effectiveness and develops improvement plans and programs - contributes to the development of a high quality, committed and flexible workforce	1	2	3	4	5
6. QUALITY - contributes to the development and implementation of a total quality approach throughout the organisation - identifies, defines and meets internal customer requirements, responding quickly to their needs	1	2	3	4	5
7. SERVICE DELIVERY - anticipates requirements and set up or adapts HR-services to meet them - provides cost-effective services in each of the main areas of HRM	1	2	3	4	5
8. LEADERSHIP AND MANAGEMENT - provides excellent leadership and guidance to the members of HR-function - improves and maintains the quality of the support the function provides to line managers	1	2	3	4	5
9. INNOVATION - contributes to the development of innovation abilities of the organisation - produces annually 1-3 innovations in HRM area	1	2	3	4	5
10. CO-OPERATION - actively seeks new ways of improving co-operation at NTC and Nokia level - shares all professional knowledge among all Nokia HR colleagues	1	2	3	4	5

Fig. 5.8   An example of a competence profile of an Human Resource Director
Competence level: 5 = very good, 1 = poor

- One of the biggest challenges for the human resource professionals is supporting continuous change, and it is expected to remain so in the years ahead.
- Connecting human resource work to the strategy of the organisation is one of the most important issues and will be a special challenge in a change situation.
- Competence management is emphasised in the future for the following reasons:

- the significance of competence as a competitive factor;
- age structure; and
- competition in the work force.
- The speed of change creates pressure on competence management and how it affects objective setting and planning and development discussions.
- Well-being and the control of age structure are key questions in all kinds of organisations.

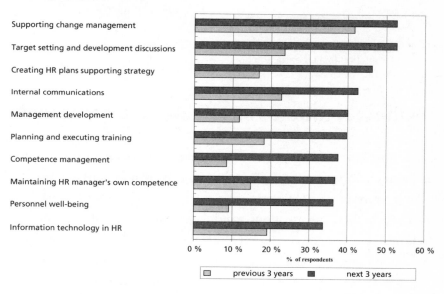

Fig. 5.9   The focus areas of human resource management in Finland according to a survey by PA Consulting Group

In an intelligent organisation the role of the human resource function will be transformed into a trend-setting function. Figure 5.10 shows how the human resource function has developed over the years. In the 70s it was mainly an administrative function, in the 80s a service function and in the 90s a support function. From now on its role could evolve in the direction of steering and trend-setting. Previously people were expected to adapt according to the needs of the companies and markets. More attention will hopefully be attached to individuals in the future: the roles will be reversed so that companies and work-places will be shaped according to the needs of the individuals. The employees will have a key role in the development of the organisation's operations.

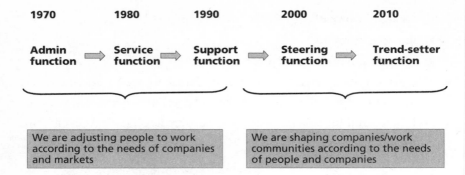

Fig. 5.10   The development of the human resource function from an administrative function to a steering function

On the way towards an intelligent organisation

Below I present two examples of organisations that are clearly on the way to becoming truly intelligent organisations. These organisations are described from the perspective of human resource management. In other words, I will discuss how these organisations acquire, develop and maintain competent and committed employees. I want to use the examples to show that human resource management can have a very practical impact on business.

The two examples have some points in common, all of which are critical in the implementation of successful human resource management. They are:

- Employees are really regarded as the most important resource and the company is ready to invest in their competence and wellbeing.
- Top management is committed to and actively involved in the development of human resource management.
- Human resource management is based on a clear model that helps steer operations and define the focus areas.
- Line managers have the main responsibility in the implementation of human resource management.
- Human resource processes are clearly described and the tools are simple.
- Human resource management is done systematically and on a long term basis.

- The results of human resource management are measured systematically.
- The roles and duties of those participating in human resource management – top management, line managers, human resource people and employees – are specified in detail.

Nokia's Fixed Access Systems Division (FAS)

At the end of the 90s, the FAS division employed approximately 3000 people globally. The division grew quickly during the period 1994–1997. Operations expanded and internationalised strongly, which meant that the successful recruitment and selection of managers played a vital role. There were product development units in Espoo, Oulu, Haukipudas, Cambridge, Düsseldorf, Boston and Melbourne. There were production plants in Oulu, Haukipudas and China.

The task areas of the human resource department are shown in Fig. 5.11. As you can see, the duties were very versatile and there were plenty of them. The human resource department of FAS also included office services and real estate services that are not included in the picture, since they do

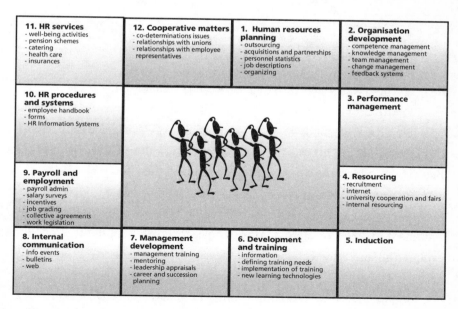

Fig. 5.11   The task areas of the human resource department

not normally belong to the duties of the human resource department. But the human resource department was a typical service function in that it was continuously getting different kinds of requests from various parts of the organisation. In these circumstances prioritising was essential.

The human resource strategy of FAS is shown in Fig. 5.12. At that time, its primary aim was to support the development and maintenance of an efficient, learning and healthy organisation. All the department's operations were supposed to somehow improve these three factors. Where they didn't it was fair to ask whether the operation had a meaningful role. One principle was also: the less paperwork the better.

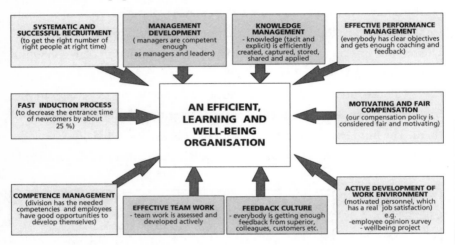

Fig. 5.12 The basic elements of the human resource strategy of FAS

Figure 5.12 also shows the ten focus areas. As you can see from the task areas, there is a lot to do, so it is important to give priorities and to concentrate on the essentials – the things that bring value to the organisation. Below I describe some concrete projects from all these focus areas.

Recruitment was of one of the key areas at that time. We needed to hire new experts fast and were constantly trying to improve and speed up the recruitment process. We started, for example, advertising on the Internet and explored all sorts of new channels. Info sessions were organised for the managers so that they would be trained for their own role in the recruitment process.

Job induction was also important. The general objective was to shorten the induction period of a newcomer by about 25 percent. In practice this was done by trimming the process, training the managers, developing the material and by efficient practical organisation of job orientation. The quality of the induction process was monitored by a survey conducted among the newcomers twice a year.

Competence management was another of the key areas. In practice, this meant that the necessary competence would be evaluated twice a year on the division, department, team and individual levels and development plans would be made. The general target was that the employees would have plenty of opportunity to develop their own competence. We tried to use new training technologies, set up learning centres and arranged 'learn how to learn' training courses.

Heavy investment was made in performance management. The idea was that everyone would have clear objectives and would receive enough coaching and feedback. Each person had the right to a planning and development discussion twice a year. Both superiors and subordinates were always offered a chance to get training on it just before the discussion round started. The implementation and quality of the discussions was followed by a survey sent to the managers twice a year. We wanted to make sure that the dicussions would actually take place and that people were prepared for any possible pitfalls that might arise.

Motivation and a fair rewarding system was also one of the key areas. Our general aim was that the employees would feel that their salary level and other fringe benefits were appropriate. Salary issues were as open as possible while respecting the principle of individual salary secrecy. Managers were trained and given new tools to deal with questions about compensation.

The sixth key area was the active development of the work community. We wanted motivated, committed, and contented employees. We used a fairly extensive annual employee survey (about 60 questions) to monitor that ambition. The results were then assessed on the departmental, unit and divisional level. Development plans were made within the context of the results and their implementation was closely watched. There was also a 'total wellness' project that concentrated on things like:

* emphasising the significance of total wellness and everyone's own responsibility of balancing his/her own life;

- offering opportunity for different hobbies;
- arranging different events, like sports days, fitness tests, theatre visits; and
- organising general lectures by well-known experts from different areas (writers, philosophers, actors, etc.).

The results of the employee survey did a good job of describing the state of play in the different areas. We drafted a so-called satisfaction index on the basis of the results. This index developed very encouragingly between 1996 and 1999. In 1996 the index was 60.3 percent and by 1999 it had increased to 64.1 percent. One factor behind the improvement was the systematic invest-ment in human resource management in the whole division.

We paid special attention to management development from the start. My boss said that it was the most important project underway when I started at Nokia. In 1994–1997 we implemented an extensive training programme for managers made up of four modules and lasting 11 days. More than 200 managers participated in the training programme (10 courses). The idea was to quickly improve the basic readiness of managers. The competence of the more experienced managers was improved with the help of the so-called Black Book project. Management was actively assessed and training in human resource issues was organised for managers. We also tried mentoring in the development of managers. That meant a more experienced department man-ager leading a group of 3–5 younger managers. The group was supposed to try to learn something new and to solve a new problem every day.

Teamwork was intensified. We defined a common teamwork concept and organised training on teamwork. We even developed an evaluation form for teamwork. Teams drafted their own development plan in response to these evaluations. And the management group evaluated their own op-erations and organised a one-day team training session.

We also wanted to invest in the development of a feedback culture so that everyone would receive enough feedback from his or her superior, sub-ordinates, colleagues, and customers. A one-day training seminar was ar-ranged on feedback for all managers. We started from analysis of the em-ployee survey from 1996. The survey had found that only 39 percent of employees were satisfied with the following thesis: 'I get enough feedback from my superior.' This made us consider the significance of feedback in a wider sense and on that basis we started to work on the feedback culture in the whole division.

The last focus area was knowledge management. Here the target was to make sure that knowledge was created, captured, stored, shared and applied efficiently. In the early phase our training worked to make the employees familiar with the concept and then we implemented some pilot projects that were described earlier in the chapter 'Knowledge Management'.

I think we succeeded fairly well. The key factors in our success were:

- Strong commitment of the management to development. My superior perfectly understood the significance of human resource management. And the whole management group was actively involved in the development of human resource management.
- The clear vision and framework of human resource management helped to define the basic structure and steer our operations.
- Things were done systematically and persistently. We also tried to measure as many things as possible.
- The human resource department enjoyed its work and worked well as a team. Moreover, the support of Nokia Telecommunications' human resource department was massive.
- The period 1995–1998 was fairly stable (on a Nokia scale).

When FAS decided it needed to overhaul itself in 1999, we embarked on another round of serious change. A product line, a production plant and a smaller production unit of the division were sold and some functions were outsourced. Two smaller companies were bought from the United States and one plant and product development unit was set up. The management of the division moved to California and the number of employees dropped from 3000 to 1000. Behind all this was a big reorganisation of the division's strategy. Fixed Access Systems was buried and replaced by Broadband Systems Division. From the viewpoint of human resource management it was a great relief that, in spite of all these numerous change projects, a new job was found for every employee. It suggests that at least we had taken good care of the employees' competence.

The Technical Research Centre of Finland (VTT)

The Technical Research Centre of Finland (VTT) has a staff of around 3000 and provides technical and techno-economic research services. In 1999 VTT's total turnover was 201 million euros. About 70% of the firm's income was generated by research in the domestic private and public sector and abroad. Budget funding accounted for roughly 30% of turnover and was directed to VTT's own strategic research.

VTT's vision is to be a world leader in technology research and to benefit the whole of Finland by its excellence. This vision consists of three strategic objectives: to take its competitiveness to a new and truly international level, to make VTT a world-class brand, and to implement exemplary working methods that help boost employee satisfaction.

Realising this vision requires a systematic approach to human resource management and management development, as well as purposeful implementation of plans. In other words, there is no hope of success without a clear personnel policy and strategy.

Through its personnel policy and strategy, VTT has tried to ensure it has the levels of performance and expertise it needs to make its plans realisable. One of the most important challenges of this policy has been keeping its staff motivated to continually develop their skill set and strive to improve their performance. This means sorting out:

- how they agree about goals and enhance their realisation;
- how they appraise performance, give feedback, support development and reward performance; and
- how they measure and improve job satisfaction and employees' commitment.

VTT's personnel policy has specified a certain minimum level of personnel management but, in a competitive situation, it clearly needs to aim to go further. That is why it needs a personnel strategy and, moving beyond that, development goals for every individual situation.

Division of duties in human resources management

VTT is managed as a results-oriented organisation. Each profit unit is responsible for the management and development of its own personnel in order to ensure it can match the expertise and performance levels demanded by the firm's strategic plans. The group level (management group and personnel director) creates the environment for human resource management, and provides support for the process of securing the required skills and performance levels.

The current division of responsibilities between the profit units and the group can be described in brief as in Fig. 5.13.

Personnel Management Processes in VTT

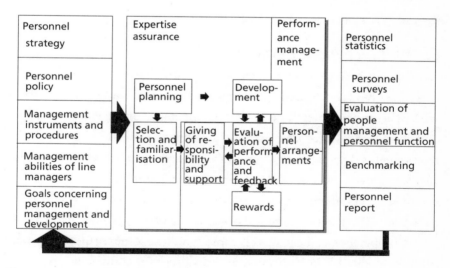

Fig. 5.13   Personnel management process at VTT

VTT's line managers are responsible for the processes described in the central area of the graph, starting from personnel planning and ending with personnel arrangements. In this they are supported by the environment and HR specialists.

The annual personnel report forms a link to short and long-term goal-setting (see Fig. 5.14). It assesses and summarises the quantity and quality of human resources within the working community.

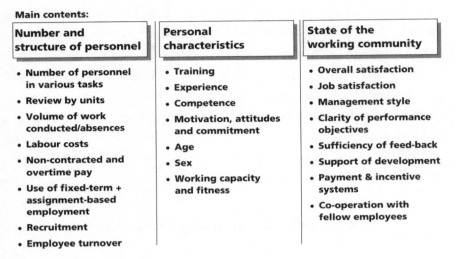

Main contents:

Number and structure of personnel	Personal characteristics	State of the working community
• Number of personnel in various tasks • Review by units • Volume of work conducted/absences • Labour costs • Non-contracted and overtime pay • Use of fixed-term + assignment-based employment • Recruitment • Employee turnover	• Training • Experience • Competence • Motivation, attitudes and commitment • Age • Sex • Working capacity and fitness	• Overall satisfaction • Job satisfaction • Management style • Clarity of performance objectives • Sufficiency of feed-back • Support of development • Payment & incentive systems • Co-operation with fellow employees

Fig. 5.14 VTT´s annual personnel report

Competence management at VTT

Competence management, especially being sure that, looking forward, the employees have the desired competencies and skills, is an essential part of VTT's personnel strategy and success. Competence management is a process where each research unit, area and group refines the future competence requirements dictated by strategy and assesses the gap between the current and target levels. After that, development discussions are used to agree on personal development targets and supporting needs. The process also includes recruiting, networking and outsourcing plans (see Fig. 5.15).

Competence management is more than just some form of quantitative and qualitative identification and definition of competence needs. It is necessary to establish the employees' own career and life goals and the true extent to which they are willing to commit and discuss these needs and expectations in order to make a deal of development and support. It's also important to be better and better at organising learning and strengthening

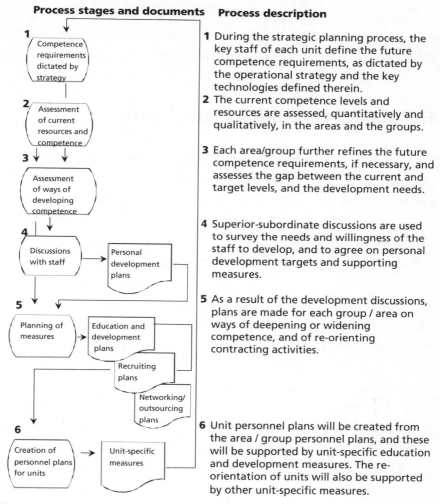

Process stages and documents   **Process description**

1 During the strategic planning process, the key staff of each unit define the future competence requirements, as dictated by the operational strategy and the key technologies defined therein.

2 The current competence levels and resources are assessed, quantitatively and qualitatively, in the areas and the groups.

3 Each area/group further refines the future competence requirements, if necessary, and assesses the gap between the current and target levels, and the development needs.

4 Superior-subordinate discussions are used to survey the needs and willingness of the staff to develop, and to agree on personal development targets and supporting measures.

5 As a result of the development discussions, plans are made for each group / area on ways of deepening or widening competence, and of re-orienting contracting activities.

6 Unit personnel plans will be created from the area / group personnel plans, and these will be supported by unit-specific education and development measures. The re-orientation of units will also be supported by other unit-specific measures.

Fig. 5.15   Competence management process at VTT

the characteristics of a learning organisation. These are now the main challenges of competence management at VTT.

Summary

VTT has accepted the challenge of putting its personnel and people at the centre in its attempt to reach the requisite level of competence and performance. It has a model for continuously improving human resources and HR management. And at the heart of this model are the roles of the different actors, the continuous improvement of HR approaches and leadership skills, short and long-term goals and their measurement, and an annual personnel report as a basis of discussions and decision-making in top management.

The ideal organisation of the future

The ideal organisation of the future is efficient, learning and healthy. It is intelligent and knows how to balance these factors correctly. It has the ability to renew itself continuously and to foresee changes. Organisational learning is faster than the changes in the environment and this is why it is able to manage change. Employees are its most important resource and therefore it is structured to pay close attention to their well-being.

We should build organisations for people, not adapt people to organisations. We should have a vision about our work communities, too. We spend the best part of our lives in different organisations. We should make these organisations ideal places to work in, be together and grow comprehensively as human beings.

Is this pure idealism? Not at all. We should be able to change our idealism into realism. We should not be afraid to dream and dream of better organisations. A thought always precedes action. What we think of our work, an employee and the work community is of the utmost importance. Without idealism we are in great danger of creating mechanical machine-like organisations that exhaust their employees. Individuals burn out and organisations get paralysed. This can hardly be our future vision. The successful organisations of the future originate from today's idealism.

Living in the midst of constant change is not always fun. But we have no choice, because life is change. We are often distressed in this turbulent world. The three major reasons for this distress are:

- there are so many changes;
- the changes are so complex; and
- we are always in a hurry.

We should sometimes find time to stop and think about where we are going. But often we find ourselves just watching events unfold without an answer as to why. This affects both our working and private life. We are like boats floating along an overflowing stream. We have a hard enough job keeping our own boat afloat let alone finding the energy for anything else.

We should wake up and think what is really happening. Where are we going and who is steering our development? Is this the right direction? Are we just adapting ourselves to the changes or are we making the changes? If we do not create our own future, who is going to determine where we will have to work and live?

True change generally requires profound change in the way we think. We must build a new framework to help us to shape things differently. Only then can we really renew ourselves. This renewal is illustrated in Fig. 5.16 which shows the individual, team and organisational life cycle thinking.

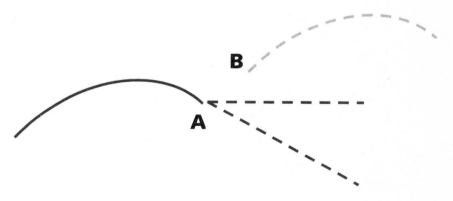

Fig. 5.16 Individual, team and organisational life cycle

Both an individual and an organisation can be in situation A shown in Fig. 5.16. There are three roads leading out of that particular situation. One is a clearly declining, regressive road that few people wish to choose, but it is where many of us end up. Then there is a straight road where life goes on according to the old model. Sooner or later this road leads to debilitating overspecialisation. The third road is the most challenging. It is the road of renewal. Getting to the road of renewal demands a radical change in thinking. We must realise the need to change, and effect that change. We must get to the new level of consciousness. The journey from A to B is not always easy. It often requires the resolution of a crisis to force change upon us. Intelligent organisations know how to renew themselves without crises.

Profound changes are not achieved without changing our thought processes. And this requires creative intelligence. We need to abandon some things. We need to leave our own comfort area. True change is like a jump into the unknown. And we must make this journey in order to be able to renew ourselves as individuals, teams and organisations. Today there is a burning need to challenge our present beliefs and create new values and ways of working. Hopefully we have enough energy, courage and wisdom to perform this task as individuals, teams and organisations.

Glossary

Key terms used in the book

Basic model of learning at work

This model offers a simple process of how we can turn our duties and daily problems or possibilities into learning experiences. With the help of systematic planning, operation, evaluation, understanding, application and transfer of what has been learnt this process aims at activating learning at work.

Competence

Competence consists of knowledge, skills, attitudes, experiences and contacts. Processes, ways of working and culture are included in organisational competence.

Competence management

Competence management means that organisational core competence or other necessary competence is defined in the context of the company vision, strategy and objectives. After this we must evaluate how the present competence level compares with the target level. The necessary development plans are drafted on this basis and then implemented and transformed into personal development plans.

Competence strategies

Competence strategies aim at achieving competitive advantage by developing competence, processes and information systems.

Core competence

Core competence is a combination of competencies, technologies and information systems that enables successful competition. Core competence is a concept used generally only on organisational level. Core competence is cumulated competence that the organisation can exploit in its present and future business when bringing added value to the customer.

Daily leadership

Daily leadership is daily steering of subordinates, supporting them, giving feedback, coaching, delegating and doing things together. Good daily leadership means that you know your subordinates, know how to lead them individually and fairly, and know how to motivate them. We can also use the term human resource management or people management.

Data

Data is raw material that constitutes information. It is numbers, text, pictures and all their combinations. Data does not contain relations or meanings, but is only separate pieces of information.

Explicit knowledge

Explicit knowledge is objective, formal, and can be easily distributed around inside the organisation.

Feedback culture

Good feedback culture consists of such factors as openness, trust, respect for the individual, generous communication, allowing mistakes, good cooperative spirit, support for others, and an emphasis on continuous learning. The feedback system does not work without compatible values.

Feedback system

The organisation's feedback system consists of different tools used to gather feedback on an individual, team and organisational level. The feedback system can be examined from the viewpoint of the feedback giver, the content of the feedback and the tools used.

Framework

A framework is a model illustrating the essential elements connected to the phenomenon and the interactive relations between these elements. The framework is helpful when we are trying to crystallise and shape the phenomenon in question comprehensively.

Human capital

Human capital is divided into three components: the number of employees, the quality of those employees, and the resulting efficiency of the work community.

Human resource strategy

Human resource strategy defines what kind of human resources the company needs in order to achieve its objectives. Human resource strategy defines, for example, issues connected to the amount, quality, location, outsourcing, competence and motivation of human resources.

Information

Information is data that has been changed into a meaningful entity in as much as it contains a message.

Intellectual capital

Intellectual capital is the sum of structural and human capital. Structural capital is divided into customer capital and organisational capital. Organisational capital, again, is divided into innovation capital, process capital, culture capital and core competence capital. Human capital is divided into three components: the number of employees, the quality of employees, and the activity of the work community.

Intelligence

Intelligence is the ability to exploit knowledge in a such a way as to be able to make the right solutions, choices and decisions. Creative intelligence is a combination of intellectual, emotional and intuitive intelligence.

Intelligent organisation

An intelligent organisation is capable of continuous renewal, able to foresee changes and learn fast. An intelligent organisation is not a mechanistic machine, but instead resembles a living organism that can steer its own operations.

Knowledge

Knowledge is a mixture of organised experiences, values, information and insights offering a framework for the evaluation of new experiences and information.

Knowledge management

Knowledge management is a process that creates, captures, stores, shares and applies knowledge. In these sub-processes individual knowledge turns into team knowledge and tacit knowledge into explicit knowledge.

Learning

Learning is a process in which the individual captures knowledge, skills, attitudes, experiences and contacts that can lead to changes in thinking, feeling or behaviour.

Learning organisation

A learning organisation has the ability to continuously adapt, change and renew itself according to the demands of the environment and it learns from its experiences and can quickly change its ways of working.

Learning styles of the individual

On the basis of their learning style people can be divided into four basic types: activist, reflector, theorist and pragmatist.

Obstacles to learning

Obstacles to learning can be examined in connection with the learning process or separately from an individual, team or organisational viewpoint. The obstacles to learning on an individual level are the analogies of a small window, thick skin, closed gate and wide river.

Organisation

An organisation is a place where people work together to form a work community. An organisation can be a company or a public association; today there are not as many differences in their form of their management as there had been in the past.

Organisational learning

Organisational learning means the organisation's ability to renew itself by changing its processes and ways of working. Renewal means in practice that the organisation is ready to acquire new competence continuously and exploit it immediately.

Organisational learning skills

Organisational learning skills are the organisation's ways of working, processes and values that influence the efficiency of organisational learning.

Management by interaction

Management by interaction is a management philosophy and thinking model that identifies the need to manage the ever more complicated interactive relationships as a key success factor in the strategic management of companies in the future.

Paradigm

Paradigms or prevalent beliefs and thinking models are frameworks through which we observe our environment. Scientists talk about the picture of the world and business management consultants about the prevailing logic. Thus paradigms work as filters steering our thinking. It is dangerous if our decisions are still guided by an outmoded belief system that has become detached from reality.

Performance management

Performance management combines an agreement on objectives, coaching, result evaluation, and development as elements connected to each other in a continuous process designed to improve the performance of the organisation by developing individuals and teams. Performance management means most simply that everyone knows their duty, their personal objectives, what kind of competence is required of them, and that they get enough coaching and feedback in order to be able to take care of their duties.

Personal development plan

Individual training and development needs are defined in the personal development plan. The schedule of different development measures for the next six months is included in this plan.

Planning and development discussions

A planning and development discussion is a systematic and regular talk (normally twice a year) between the manager and the employee (subordinate) aiming at improving performance and promoting open communication.

Planning meetings

Planning meetings are an important part of performance management on the department level. In these meetings the whole crowd is engaged in planning, setting targets, following the implementation of objectives, defining critical competencies and making development plans.

Process

A process is a chain of actions linked to each other starting from the need of the customer and ends in meeting the customer's need. Main and support processes are separated from each other.

Reflection

Reflection is the thorough evaluation of things with the aim of understanding them and the relationship they have with other things.

Staircase of learning

Learning is knowing, understanding, applying and developing.

Strategic management

Strategic management is a continuous process including the compilation of the strategy, strategic planning, implementation, evaluation and updating. The whole staff participates in this form of management. The strategy consists of a group of decisions, choices and measures that the organisation uses in order to achieve its goals. The strategy is divided into strategic positioning and strategic resources.

Tacit knowledge

Tacit knowledge is not documented and is difficult to transfer to others.

Team

A team is a small group of people who have competencies complementing each other. The team is committed to a common objective, common performance targets and a common action model. The team also feels that it is jointly responsible for its performance.

Team learning

Team learning is a process in which the team captures new knowledge, skills, attitudes, experiences and contacts leading to changes in its operations.

Transformation

A profound change in the organisation taking place on the level of the company vision, its values and beliefs.

Types of learning

There are four different types of learning: reactive learning, predictive learning, action learning and questioning learning.

Vision

A vision describes the organisation's state of intent in a certain time span.

References

Aaltonen, Tapio and Junkkari, Lari (1999) *Yrityksen arvot ja etiikka*, WSOY.

ABB Production Technology. (1999) *Building Future Competitiveness from Competence Management to Knowledge Management and Beyond*, ABB Corporate Research Oy.

Ahonen, Guy (1998) *Henkilöstötilinpäätös. Yrityksen ikkuna menestykselliseen tulevaisuuteen*, Kauppakaari.

Ajahn Sumano, Bhikkhu (1999) *Questions from the City, Answers from the Forest. Simple Lessons You Can Use from a Western Buddhist Monk*, Quest Books, Wheaton.

Bacal, Robert (1999) *Performance Management*, McGraw Hill, New York.

Bennis, Warren and Parikh, Jagdish and Lessem, Ronnie (1995) *Beyond Leadership. Balancing Economics, Ethics and Ecology*, Revised Edition, Blackwell. Oxford.

Blanchard, Ken and O'Connor, Michael. (1997) *Managing by Values*, Berret-Koehler Publishers. San Francisco.

Broad, Mary L and Newstrom, John W. (1992) *Transfer of Training. Action-Packed Strategies to Ensure High Payoff from Training Investments*, Addison Wesley.

Brooking, Annie (1997) *Intellectual Capital. Core Asset for the Third Millenium Enterprise*, International Thomson Business Press.

Davenport, Thomas H. and Prusak, Laurence (1998) *Working Knowledge. How Organisations Manage What They Know*, Harvard Business School Press, Boston.

Davenport, Thomas H. (2000) *Mission Critical. Realizing the Promise of Enterprise Systems*, Harvard Business School Press, Boston.

De Geus, Arie (1997) *The Living Company. Growth, Learning and Longevity in Business*, Nicholas Brealey Publishing.

Deevy, Edward (1995) *Creating the Resilient Organization. A Rapid Response Management Program*, Prentice Hall, Englewood Cliffs.

Dibella, Anthony J. and Nevis, Edwin C. (1998) *How Organizations Learn. An Integrated Strategy for Building Learning Capability*, Jossey-Bass Publishers.

Dubois, David D. (1993) *Competency-based Performance Improvement. A Strategy for Organizational Change*, HRD Press.

Easterby-Smith, Mark and Burgoynne, John and Araujo, Luis (1999) *Organizational Learning and the Learning Organization. Developments in Theory and Practice*, SAGE Publications.

Edwards, Mark R. and Ewen, Ann J. *360 Feedback. The Powerful New Model for Employee Assessment and Performance Improvement*, Amacom.

Edvindsson, Leif and Malone, Michael (1997) *Intellectual Capital*, Harper Business.

Eronen, Anne (1997) *Henkilöstön osaaminen yrityksen taseeseen?* ETLA. Elinkeinoelämän Tutkimuskeskus, Helsinki.

Gilbert, Thomas F. (1996) *Human Competence. Engineering Worthy Performance. Tribute Edition*, The International Society for Performance Improvement.

Goleman, Daniel (1995) *Emotional Intelligence. Why it can matter more than IQ*, Bamtam Books.

Gratton, Lynda (2000) *Living Strategy. Putting People at the Heart of Corporate Purpose*, Pearson Education, London.

Guns, Bob (1996) *The Faster Learning Organization. Gain and Sustain the Competitive Edge*, Pfeiffer & Company.

Hamel, Gary and Prahalad, C.K. (1994) *Competing for the Future. Breakthrough Strategies for Seizing Control of Your Industry and Creating the Markets of Tomorrow*, Harvard Business School Press.

Hammer, Michael and Champy James (1993) *Reengineering the Corporation. A Manifesto for Business Revolution*, Nicholas Brealey Publishing.

Hannus, Jouko and Lindroos, Jan-Erik and Seppänen, Tapani (1999) *Strateginen uudistuminen osaamisen ajan toimintaympäristössä*, HM&V Research Oy.

Hannus, Jouko (1993) *Prosessijohtaminen. Ydinprosessien uudistamien ja yrityksen suorityukyky. Toinen, uudistettu pianos*, HM&V Research Oy.

Hax, Arnoldo C. and Mailuf, Nicolas S. *The Strategy Concept and Process. A Pragmatic Approach*, Prentice Hall.

Hersey, Paul and Blanchard, Kenneth H. (1990) *Tilannejohtaminen. Tuloksiin ihmisten avulla*, Gummerus.

Honey, Peter and Mumford, Alan (1992) *The Manual of Learning Styles*, Third Editon.

Hope, Jeremy and Hope, Tony (1998) *Kolmannen aallon kilpailu. Kymmenen avainaluetta tietoajan yritysten johtamisessa*, WSOY, Porvoo.

Hätönen, Heljä (1998) *Osaava henkilöstö-nyt ja tulevaisuudessa*, Metalliteollisuuden Keskusliitto.

Juch, Bert (1983) *Personal Development. Theory and Practice in Management Training*, John Wiley & Sons.

Kamensky, Mika (2000) *Strateginen johtaminen*, Kauppakaari.

Katzenbach, Jon R and Smith, Douglas K. (1994) *The Wisdom of Teams. Creating the High-Performance Organization*, Harvard Business School Press.

Kirkpatrick, Donald L. (1994) *Evaluating Training Programs. The four levels*, Berrett-Koehler Publishers.

Kline, Peter and Sauders, Bernard (1998) *Ten Steps to a Learning Organization*, Great Ocean Publishers.

Koestenbaum, Peter. (1991) *Leadership. The Inner Side of Greatness. A Philosophy for Leaders*, Jossey-Bass Publishers.

Kolb, Donald (1984. *Experiential Learning. Experience as the Source of Learning and Development*, Prentice Hall, Inc.

Koski, Jussi T. (1998) *Infoähky ja muita kirjoituksia oppimisesta, organisaatioista ja tietoyhteiskunnasta*, Gummerus.

Kulkki, Seija and Kosonen, Mikko. (1999) *How Tacit Knowledge Explains Organizational Renewal and Growth: The Case of Nokia*. To be published in: Nonaka, Ikuro and Tecce, David (eds.) *Knowledge Creation and the Firm*, SAGE Publication Press, (forthcoming).

Lahti, Kari (1991. *Oppimis-ja toimintatyylit*, Moniste, Psyko Oy.

Lepsinger, Richard and Lucia, Anntoinette D. (1997) *The Art and Science of 360 Feedback*, Jossey-Bass Pfeiffer.

Lessem, Ronnie and Sudhanshu, Palsule (1997) *Managing in Four Worlds. From Competition to Co-creation*, Blackwell, Oxford.

Marquardt, Michael and Reynolds, Angus (1994) *Global Learning Organization. Gaining Competitive Advantage through Continuous Learning*, IRWIN Professional Publishing.

Marquardt, Michael J. (1996) *Building the Learning Organisation*, McGraw-Hill.

Mayo, Andrew and Lank, Elizabeth (1994) *The Power of Learning. A Guide to Gaining Competive Advantage*, Institute of Personnel and Development.

Mayo, Andrew (1991) *Managing Careers. Strategies for Organizations*, Institute of Personal Management.

Mellander, Klas (1993) *The Power of Learning. Fostering Employee Growth*, ASTD.

Myers, Paul S. (Ed) (1996) *Knowledge Management and Organizational Design*, Butterworth-Heinemann.

Mäkelin, Matti and Vepsäläinen, Ari P. J. (1994) *Kilpailu kyvykkyydellä. Teknologia-, tuotanto- ja markkinointistrategiat*, HM&V Research Oy.

Mäkinen, Marko (1995) *Nokia Saga. Kertomus yrityksestä ja ihmisistä, jotka muuttivat sen*, Gummerus.

Nonaka, Ikujiro and Takeuchi, Hirotaka (1995) *The Knowledge-Creating Company. How Japanise Companies Create the Dynamics of Innovation*, Oxford University Press, New York.

Otala, Leenamaija (1996) *Oppimisen etu-Kilpailukykyä muutoksessa*, WSOY.

Owen, Harrison (1991) *Riding the Tiger: Doing Business in a Transforming World*, Abbott Publishing.

Parikh, Jagdish (1999) *Managing Relationships. Making a Life While Making a Living*, Capstone.

Pedler, Mike and Burgoyne, John and Boydell, Tom (1997) *The Learning Company. A Strategy for Sustainable Development*, Second Edition, The McGraw-Hill Companies.

Robinson, Dana Gaines and Robinson, James C. (1989) *Training for Impact. How to Link Training to Business Needs and Measure the Results*, Jossey-Bass Publishers.

Robinson, Dana Gaines and Robinson, James C. (1995) *Performance Consulting. Moving Beyond Training*, Berret-Koehler Publishers.

Ruggless, III, Rudy L. (Editor) (1997) *Knowledge Management Tools*, Butterworth-Heinemann.

Ruohotie, Pekka (1996) *Oppimalla osaamiseen ja menestykseen*, Edita.

Sarala, Urpo and Sarala, Anita (1996) *Oppiva organisaatio. Oppimisen, laadun ja tuottavuuden parantaminen. Helsingin yliopiston Lahden tutkimus- ja koulutuskeskus.*

Sattelberger, Thomas (Hrsg.) (1994) *Die Lernende Organisationen. Konzepte für eine neue Qualität der Unternehmensentwicklung*, Gabler.

Savage, Charles M. (1990) *5th Generation Management. Integrating Enterprises through Human Networking*, Digital Press.

Schank, Roger (1997) *Virtual Learning. A Revolutionary Approach to Building a Highly Skilled Workforce*, McGraw Hill, New York.

Senge, Peter (1990) *The Fifth Discipline. The Art and Practise of the Learning Organization*, Doubleday.

Spencer, Lyle M. Jr. and Spencer, Signe M. (1993) *Competence at Work. Models for Superior Performance*, John Wiley & Sons Inc.

Stewart, Thomas A. (1997) *Intellectual Capital. The New Wealth of Organizations*, Nicholas Brealey Publishing.

Ståhle Pirjo ja Grönroos Mauri, (1999) *Knowledge Management*, WSOY.

Sveiby, Karl Erik (1997) *The New Organizational Wealth. Managing and Measuring Knowledge Based Assets*, Berret-Koehler Publishers, San Francisco.

Tahvanainen, Marja. (1998) *Expatriate Performance Management. The Case of Nokia Telecommunications*, Doctoral Dissertation, Helsinki School of Economics and Business Administration.

Ulrich, Dave (1997) *Human Resource Champions. The next Agenda for Adding Value and Deliviring Results*, Harvard Business School, Boston.

Weiss, Tracey B. and Franklin, Hartle (1997) *Reengineering Performance Management. Breakthroughs in Achieving Strategy Through People*, The Hay Group.

Verkasalo, Matti (1997) *On the Efficient Distribution of Expert Knowledge in a Business Environment*, Department of Electrical Engineering. University of Oulu.

Wilson, Thomas B. (1995) *Innovative Reward Systems for the Changing Workplace*, McGraw-Hill, Inc.

Wyburd, Giles (1998) *Competitive and Ethical. How Business Can Strike a Balance*, Kogan Page. London.

Zohar, Danah (1997) *ReWiring the Corporate Brain. Using the New Science to Rethink How We Structure and Lead Organizations*, Berret-Koehler Publishers, San Francisco.

Appendix 1

NOKIA

PERFORMANCE MANAGEMENT
PLANNING AND DEVELOPMENT DISCUSSION

☐ **EVALUATION REVIEW**
☐ **OBJECTIVES SETTING**
☐ **DEVELOPMENT REVIEW**

The Planning and Development Discussion is a systematic and regular (normally twice a year) talk between the employee and the manager in order to improve performance and open communication.

The objectives of the development discussion are to:

1. Evaluate the results achieved
2. Set objectives for the next period
3. Define development needs and make an individual development plan
4. Develop the co-operation between the superior and the subordinate
5. Enhance general working conditions

NAME:
POSITION:
DEPARTMENT/UNIT:
PLANNING PERIOD
REVIEW PERIOD:

A. Meeting personal objectives

How successful has the employee´s performance been when weighed against the objectives set for the period?

Key results and an estimate of achievement against objectives

* Performance rating

1. _____ ☐
2. _____ ☐
3. _____ ☐
4. _____ ☐
5. _____ ☐
6. _____ ☐
7. _____ ☐
8. _____ ☐
9. _____ ☐
10. _____ ☐

Overall rating on the achievement of results ☐

B. General performance, e.g. contribution to work of others, attitude, communication, organisational skills etc.

* Rating Scale
1. Unsatisfactory (performance unacceptable at this level)
2. Fair (some aspects of performance below requirements)
3. Good (fully effective)
4. Excellent (exceeds requirements)
5. Outstanding

EVALUATION REVIEW

C. Factors which have contributed to the achievement of objectives,
e.g. resources and authorisation, environmental factors, manager's performance, employee's own performance:

D. Factors which have obstructed to the achievement of objectives,
e.g: resources and authorisation, environmental factors, manager's performance, employee's own performance:

E. The way of acting in an intelligent organisation / the values
How do you see these 12 aspects of the values of the organisation are reflected in A) your own behavior B) your manager's behavior C) generally in your department. Both the employee and the manager should give their evaluation beforehand and then analyse it together in their discussion. After that it is very important to define some action points as to how to improve the situation. The purpose of including the values in PD-discussion is to make them more concrete in the everyday working environment and constantly develop the organisation.

Please use the scale from previous page

no	Criterion	Employee	Manager	Department
	CUSTOMER SATISFACTION			
1	Discovering customer needs	1 2 3 4 5	1 2 3 4 5	1 2 3 4 5
2	Respecting and caring for the customers	1 2 3 4 5	1 2 3 4 5	1 2 3 4 5
	RESPECT FOR THE INDIVIDUAL			
3	Fair treatment on all occasions	1 2 3 4 5	1 2 3 4 5	1 2 3 4 5
4	Acceptance of diversity	1 2 3 4 5	1 2 3 4 5	1 2 3 4 5
	TEAM WORK			
5	Appreciation of team work	1 2 3 4 5	1 2 3 4 5	1 2 3 4 5
6	Supporting other team members	1 2 3 4 5	1 2 3 4 5	1 2 3 4 5
	ACHIEVEMENT			
7	Shared vision and goals	1 2 3 4 5	1 2 3 4 5	1 2 3 4 5
8	Feedback and appreciation	1 2 3 4 5	1 2 3 4 5	1 2 3 4 5
	KNOWLEDGE SHARING			
9	Active sharing of knowledge	1 2 3 4 5	1 2 3 4 5	1 2 3 4 5
10	Independent searching of new knowledge	1 2 3 4 5	1 2 3 4 5	1 2 3 4 5
	CONTINUOUS LEARNING			
11	Innovativeness and courage	1 2 3 4 5	1 2 3 4 5	1 2 3 4 5
12	Humble and open mind	1 2 3 4 5	1 2 3 4 5	1 2 3 4 5

What are the three most important action points based on the above analysis?
1. _____
2. _____
3. _____

OBJECTIVE SETTING

A.   Job description / purpose of the job

Briefly define why this job exists? Think also about how it will change in the future. The present job description should also be updated if there have been major changes to the function.

B.   Key task areas (in parenthesis the time amount in percentage)

Key task areas are the most important areas of the job for which the employee is responsible. Include here also process and matrix task areas for the next planning period.

1.
2.
3.
4.
5.
6.
7.
8.
9.
10.

C. Key objectives

From the key task areas the manager and the employee work jointly to agree key objectives and measures for the next planning period (6 months).

1.

2.

3.

4.

5.

6.

7.

8.

9.

10.

D. Key competencies for the job

What knowledge, skills, attitudes, experiences and contacts are necessary to achieve good results?

Knowledge:

Skills:

Attitudes:

Experiences and contacts:

DEVELOPMENT REVIEW *

A. Employee´s own objectives and opinions

Job satisfaction, working atmosphere, expectations regarding manager´s performance

Other work-related expectations and long-term plans for the future, e.g. areas of interest, job rotation plans

Employee´s own personal situation and plans, e.g. plans or wishes to move to another location

B. Manager´s expectations

How the employee can improve his/her performance and develop him/herself, e.g. in relation to core capabilities for the job.

*This part of the PD discussion should be conducted once a year more thoroughly. The other discussion could be more of a follow-up of agreed actions.

Appendix 2

PERFORMANCE MANAGEMENT

PLANNING AND DEVELOPMENT DISCUSSION / SHORT VERSION

Planning and development discussion is a common tool for manager and employee to use to improve performance, competencies and general working conditions.

The objective is that every employee should have this kind of planning and development discussion once a year.

The objectives of the planning and development discussion are:

      1. To meet and learn to know each other better.

      2. To clarify the goals of the department and clarify also the employee´s chances of meeting these goals.

      3. To ensure that everyone is performing well.

      4. To develop cooperation within and between different departments.

This form is a check-list for the discussion. The discussion can have also oher topics but at least these topics should be discussed. There are plenty of room for notes. Common agreements should be documented so we remember next time what was agreed previously. This way the discussion will be a true development process. You need about 45 minutes to an hour for the discussion.

Name: _____

Job: _____ Department: _____ Superior: _____

Date: _____

---

1. PERSONAL MATTERS (employee's work-related matters: eg. life situation, family, training, hobbies etc.)

_____
_____
_____
_____

2. SITUATION IN THE DEPARTMENT

In items 2.1. to 2.5.it is especially important to reflect how the employee could affect these

2.1. The objectives of the department (Quantitative and qualitative objectives will be discussed and the reality of the objectives will be checked).

_____
_____
_____

2.2. Feedback about an employee´s performance (what things went well, where there is room for improvement)

Employee:_____

Manager: _____

2.3. Cooperation and climate in the department (How the employee sees the working climate and cooperation with other colleagues, manager and other departments.)

_____
_____
_____

2.4 The implementation of values.
(How the values are implemented by employee, manager and the whole department . (E = excellent, G = good, F = fair, U =unsatisfasctory))

	Employee	Manager	Department
Customer satisfaction *			
Continuous learning			
Achievement			
Respect for the individual			

* Internal and external customers

2.5. What is your impact on the improvement of quality? (circle the right alternative)

E = excellent   G = good   F = fair   U = unsatisfactory

Reasons:

_____

_____

3. DEVELOPMENT AND MULTICOMPETENCY IN THE JOB
(What kind of competencies can you develop? How could you widen and change the content of your job?)

3.1. Actions and timetable for your personal development plan.

What kind of competencies?

_____

_____

How to develop ?

_____

_____

3.2. Actions and timetable for improving multicompetency

What kind of multicompetency is needed?

_____

_____

How to develop?

_____

_____

3.3. Actions and timetable to broaden the content of job

_____

_____

_____

In addition, the following was agreed together:

_____

_____

Appendix 3

PLANNING AND DEVELOPMENT DISCUSSION OF A TEAM

NAME OF TEAM: _____

UNIT/DEPARTMENT:_____

NAME OF THE MANAGER AND JOB:_____
(The direct superior of team, e.g.Team Leader)

APPROVAL OF THE SUPERIOR:_____
(After filling the form the superior and a team members approve it by signing)

Names of team members:		Approved

NEED TO BE UPDATED AT THE LATEST: _____

Teams have a planning and development discussion with the direct superior at least once a year and always when working conditions undergo a fundamental change. Unless otherwise agreed, this form should be updated after one year at the latest.

The objectives of a team are agreed, when every member of a team and the supervisor have signed this form.

A.   THE MAIN PURPOSE OF A TEAM

Define with a one sentence why a team exists? What is the vision of a team?

B.   TEAM´S CUSTOMERS

Who are the customers? What kind of products and services does a team offer for them? In addition to external customers a team has also internal customers, e.g. a team performing the next phase. Team´s customers are everyone a team offers services and products.

Customer:	Team´s product and service:

Whose customer is a team? Who is suppling products or services to a team? Supplier is e.g. a team performing the previous work phase.

Supplier:	The product or service a team gets:

C.   KEY TASKS, OBJECTIVES AND SUCCESS MEASUREMENTS

What are the most important tasks of a team? What are the objectives of a team? How do we measure the success of a team? Who is monitoring the achievement of objectives? How often?

	Task	Objective	Meter
1.			
Person following the realisation of an objective:			
2.			
Person following the realisation of an objective:			
3.			
Person following the realisation of an objective:			
4.			
Person following the realisation of an objective:			
5.			
Person following the realisation of an objective:			
6.			
Person following the realisation of an objective:			

D.   THE COMPETENCY NEEDED IN A TEAM

What kind of knowledge, skills and attitudes are necessary for a team to achieve good results? What kind of special skills are needed?

Knowledge:

Skills:

Attitudes:

E. THE WORKING CONDITIONS OF A TEAM

What kind of tools and authority does a team need to achieve it´s objectives?

Which are the possible risks? What sort of factors could prevent a team from achieving its objectives?

F. THE DEVELOPMENT PLAN OF A TEAM

How is a team developing its competency and multicompetency during the next planning period? Write down the concrete actions!

Development needs:	Persons:	Realisation:	Timetable:

G.   STEERING/COACHING OF A TEAM

How is operation of a team steered? Who or what is steering?

What a team expects from steering?

H.   THE RULES OF A TEAM

A team defines its own rules about how best to solve problem situations. These rules are always updated when needed.
In the rules, at least the following must be defined:

1) How is a team taking its decisions?
2) How is a team solving problem/crises situations?

Appendix 4

Name	Title of a job	Cost centre
Unit/Department/section		Personal number
Name and job title of the superior		

Started at present job	Directly supervises the jobs listed below:	Number of employees reporting to this position:

The main purpose of the job

Key task areas in order of importance

The knowledge and skills needed in the job	Experience needed in this job (years)
Training	Language skills

The jobs and grades of subordinates

The possible deputy job of a person

The most important connections to other functions and units in/outside the company

Authority of the employee. The employee is guided by?

AN INTELLIGENT ORGANISATION

JOB DESCRIPTION   1 (2)

Name	Title of a job	Cost centre
Unit/Department/section		Personal number
Name and job title of the superior		
Started at present job	Directly supervises the jobs listed below:	Number of employees reporting to this position:

The main purpose of the job

Key task areas in order of importance

The knowledge and skills needed in the job	Experience needed in this job (years)
Training	Language skills

The jobs and grades of subordinates

The possible deputy job of a person

The most important connections to other functions and units in/outside the company

Authority of the employee. The employee is guided by?

Appendix 5

MANAGEMENT OF YOUR JOB*

JOB DESCRIPTION/ job title/name
(=The purpose of a job. Define briefly why this job exists.)

KEY TASK AREAS (in parenthesis the time amount in percentage)

1.
2.
3.
4.
5.

6.
7.
8.
9.
10.

KEY OBJECTIVES (Ten most important objectives for the next planning period)

1.
2.
3.
4.
5.

6.
7.
8.
9.
10.

* This form enables the employee to inform the other members of the team or department about the main content of his/her job.

Index

Ahonen, Guy 160
Ala-Pietilä, Pekka 173
Alahuhta, Matti 92

Bhikkhu, Ajahn Sumano 166
Black Book 157
Bono, Edward de 31
Buzan, Tony 31

change 47–50
    factors 9–11
        amount of knowledge 9
        competition 9
        ecological well-being 9
        economic/political environment 9
        globalisation 9
        social environment/conditions 9
        technological 9
cognitive intelligence 145
competence 2, 4–5, 53
competence centres 98
competence management
    core 107
        definitions 108–9
        developing 114–15
        Finnish Broadcasting Company ex-
            ample 113–14
        Nokia example 111–13
    development
        ICL Finland example 123–7
        training department 121–3
    individual 127
        personal development plan 128
        psychological employment contract
            127
    levels 100–101
    organisational 109–11
    in practice 115–18

Nokia example 118–21
    process 97–100
    strategy 101–2, 106
        human resource management 102–3
        new thinking 103–6
    summary 129–31
    VTT example 192–3
competition 3, 5, 8–12
customer capital 158

Drucker, Peter 167

Einstein, Albert 49
Eliot, T.S. 146
emotional intelligence (EI) 48, 145
employee account 160–62
Enterprise Resource Planning 170

feedback 39, 40–46, 148, 170
Finnish Broadcasting Company (YLE)
    113–14

Geus, Aries de 11–12
globalisation 9, 138
Goleman, Daniel 48

Hamel, Gary 104, 107–9, 136
human capital 160
human resource management (HRM)
    81–2, 102–3, 141, 155–6, 170,
    178–9
    connection with performance manage-
        ment 84–8
    future focus areas 181–4
    general vision 179
    new roles 180–81

ICL Finland 118, 123–7

Idestam, Fredrik 12
information systems 40
information technology (IT) 136–7, 155, 170
intellectual capital 158–62
intelligent organisation 165–7
  features 167
    clearly defined processes 170
    continuous improvement 169
    evolving 168
    feedback 170
    human resource management 170, 178–84
    information technology 170
    investment 169–70
    management 171–8
    readiness for change 171
    renewal 168
    values 168–9
    vision and strategy 167
  future possibilities 194–6
  on the way towards 184–5
    Nokia 185–90
    Technical Research Centre of Finland 190–94
Intranet 155–6

Juch, Bert 27

Kaplan, Robert S. 104–5
KISS (keep it simple, stupid) 90
knowledge
  continuous application as objective 133–4
  described 142–6
  information 144
  intelligence 145
  management and control 145–6
  organisational flow 149–51
  tacit and explicit 137, 146–9, 156–7
    combination 147
    externalisation 147
    feedback 148
    internalisation 147–8
    socialisation 146–7
  values/beliefs 144–5
  wisdom 145
knowledge management 5, 54, 134–5
  described 138–9

factors 135–8
  best approach 137
  competence management 136
  competitive advantage 135–6
  explicit/tacit knowledge 137
  globalisation 138
  information technology 136–7
  intellectual capital 138
  process management 136
intellectual capital 158–60
  employee account 160–62
in practice 151
  action plan 154
  efficiency of distribution 156
  first steps 152–5
  Intranet application of HRM system 155–6
  IT support 155
  move from tacit to explicit 156–7
  organisational culture 154–5
  set priorities 154
  strategy to business benefits 151–2
subprocesses 139
  application 140–42
  capture 139–40
  creation 139
  sharing 140
  storing 140
summary and conclusions 162–3
Kolb model 19–22
Kone Corporation 92

Lahti, Kari 27
leadership
  daily 78–83
  self 177–8
  situational 82–3
learning 4, 7–8
  change 47
    clear vision 49
    difficulties 47–8
    efficiency 49
    slow 49
    well-being 50
  competition and survival 8–9
    change factors 9–11
    continuous renewal 12–15
    learn faster than competitors 11–12

definitions 15–28
feedback 40
   difficulty of giving 42
   importance 44–6
   meaning for individual 41–2
   organisation systems 42–4
   ten commandments 46
individual styles 22
   activist 23, 24
   pragmatist 23, 25
   reflector 23, 24
   theorist 23, 25
level 29–30
   individual 30–31
   organisational 33–4
   team 31–3
obstacles 25–8
process 19–22
   application 20–21
   experiences 19–20
   main 53–4
   reflection 20
   supportive factors 21–2
   understand 20
skills, organisational vs learning organi-
    sation 34–6
staircase 16–17
types
   action 18
   predictive 18
   reactive 17–18
   transformative 18–19
learning by doing 50–51
   basic model 51–3
learning organisation
   definitions 37
   skills 36–8
    active dialogue 40
    feedback systems 39
    information systems 40
    mental models 38
    self-management 39
    shared vision 39–40
    strategic learning 38–9
    system thinking 38
    team learning 39
   vs organisational learning 34–6
Lincoln, Abraham 169
Lönngvist, Jouko 74

management
   performance 174–7
   in practice 171–3
   self leadership 177–8
   as service function 171
   strategic 174
   visionary 173–4
management by interaction 105–6
Marquhardt, Michael 36
Montaigne, Michel de 145

NIH-syndrome (Not Invented Here) 142
Nixdorf 45
Nokia 44
   competence development 118–21
   continuous renewal 12–15
   core competencies 111–13
   Fixed Access Systems (FAS) division
    185–90
   vision management 173
Nonaka, Ikujiro 137, 148, 157
Norton, David P. 104–5

Ollila, Jorma 173
organisational capital 158
organisational learning 33–4
   vs learning organisation 34–6
Owen, Harrison 7

Parikh, Jagdish 145
performance 1–2, 4, 53
performance management 175–7
   continuous improvement as objective
    55–8
   critical success factors 90–92
   daily leadership 78–84
   links to HR processes 84
    career planning 88
    rewarding 85–7
    training and development 85
   planning and development
    contents 64–5
    different phases of discussion 68–70
    factors behind success 74–7
    objectives 63
    possible problems 70–74
    preparing for discussions 66–7
    rules of the game 68
    team discussions 77–8

planning meetings 84
self-evaluation of process 92–3
    agreeing on objectives 94
    daily leadership/coaching 93
    development plan 94
    evaluation of results 94
    general 93
    planning meetings 93
    rewarding 95
  summary 88–90
  viewpoints
    individual 60–61
    organisation 59–60
planning and development (PD) discussion
    see under performance manage-
    ment
Porter, Michael 103
Prahalad, C.K. 107–9, 136

Senge, Peter 36
Siemens 45

Siemens Nixdorf Information (SNI) sys-
    tems 45
simplicity 5–6
strategic management 174
strategy 101–7
structural capital 158

Takeuchi, Hirotaka 137, 148–9
teams 31–3, 39, 77–8, 134–5
Technical Research Centre of Finland
    (VTT) 190–91, 193–4
  competence management 192–3
  division of duties in HRM 191–2

Ulrich, David 180

Verkasalo, Matti 156
vision management 173–4
VTT *see* Technical Research Centre of Finland

YLE *see* Finnish Broadcasting Company